PRAISE FOR *MONSOON MANSION*

"In this incandescent debut memoir, Cinelle Barnes forges memories of her family's downfall with tumultuous Filipino history. Like the storm in its title, *Monsoon Mansion* immerses us in the darkest waters of memory, stirring up unbearably brutal childhood events with lyrical prose and searing imagery, forming a woven tale that is both delicate and electric. This book assures us that even when we lose those things that give shape to our humanity—our roots, culture, and family—we can go on to devise a new way of being."

—Susan Tekulve, author of *In the Garden of Stone*

"The princess becomes a pauper before she turns eleven, yet through grit and love and words, that princess, Cinelle Barnes, escapes a fallen-in mansion and broken family to survive. Light fills this beautiful memoir—breaking through the dark loneliness of a mansion with no electricity. And light will fill you and carry you on, dear reader, even after you turn the last page. *Monsoon Mansion* sings a song of rain and sparkling light, and like its author, we'll all come to know the diamonds we carry in our palms."

—Jim Minick, author of *Fire Is Your Water*

"*Monsoon Mansion* is a classic memoir that will reach every part of the world today with its personal story of love, heartbreak, betrayal, belief, and survival. An unforgettable tale of our time."

—Dan Wakefield, author of *Going All the Way* and
New York in the Fifties

MONSOON MANSION

MONSOON MANSION

A MEMOIR

Cinelle Barnes

Little
a

Published by Little A, New York

www.apub.com

Amazon, the Amazon logo, and Little A are trademarks of Amazon.com,
Inc., or its affiliates.

ISBN-13: 9781542046138 (hardcover)
ISBN-10: 1542046130 (hardcover)
ISBN-13: 9781542046145 (paperback)
ISBN-10: 1542046149 (paperback)

Cover design by Faceout Studio, Tim Green

Cover illustration by Xinmei Liu

Printed in the United States of America

First edition

For every warrior child.
And for love like the ocean.

She did not know that this was the best thing she could have done, and she did not know that, when she began to walk quickly or even run along the paths and down the avenue, she was stirring her slow blood and making herself stronger by fighting with the wind which swept down from the moor.

—Frances Hodgson Burnett, *The Secret Garden*

Contents

AUTHOR'S NOTE

Five years ago, I told my husband, "That child was a warrior and that warrior was me. That warrior child twirled and sang and drew and danced her way to freedom, and I now must tell her story." And so I decided to write a book—a work of creative nonfiction. I wanted to create beauty out of my truth. I wanted to explore the idea of hybridity in identity and in creativity. I wanted to honor the authors and characters that kept me company as a child and employ the same literary techniques I learned from these works. I wanted to craft a book of childhood trauma and of childhood magic, of grit and of beauty. What I could not remember myself, I searched through research and interviews, and confirmed details through a wide exploration of photos, videos, newspaper articles, vital records, court cases, affidavits, maps, and Google Earth.

I have changed the names of certain people, places, and businesses in order to protect those mentioned in the book and to safeguard my privacy and that of my family. On occasion, composite characters enter and exit the page, mainly because at times when I do remember faces or voices, I cannot remember names, or vice versa. In some chapters, time lapses serve the purpose of evading the superfluous. What I meant to do here was to create a mix of memory, research, and reporting told in a lyrical register reminiscent of other art forms I had previously studied: music, art history, architecture, and dance.

Reader, here is *Monsoon Mansion*, my otherworld.

Prologue

MANSION ROYALE

My parents named the house "Mansion Royale," a stately home in a post-Spanish, post-American, and newly post-Marcos democracy. They bought it together with my mother's inherited wealth and my father's new money. It was the eighties, when bigger was better, and better meant glitter, gold, and glam. Our family moved in when I was two and a half years old, in 1988, when my first narrative memories were forming. The house became the setting for the first moments of mundaneness, celebration, and terror that my developing brain could retain.

The original owners of the house had their marriage legally annulled halfway through construction and put the mansion up for sale. They left some good bones for my parents to work with. My parents paid cash for a short sale and tipped big bucks to the real estate agent, and the mansion was theirs—ours: a palace that housed Mama's social aspirations and Papa's business success and the miscellanies that were the staff, my half brother Paolo, and myself. The mansion also housed many conversations—some in English, some in Taglish (a fusion of Tagalog and English, the upper class's preferred tongue), some in straight Tagalog (the help's lingua), and a few borrowed throw-ins from Old World Spanish and island dialects.

Our family entered through wrought-iron gates that were guarded by armed security staff. Flattened metal bars curved to golden swirls sprawled from one hinge of each gate door to the other, and although outsiders could look through the gaps between the swirls, the half-ton gates kept us separate from lookers and passersby.

Past the gates, our driveway stretched from the entrance, around the front lawn, through the shaded drop-off, down to the basement parking lot, then around the back to the basketball court. When my mother threw parties, the driveway turned into a meandering buffet of shrimp cocktail, fondue, roasted whole pig, beef Wellington—and barrels, bottles, and goblets of alcohol. The winding shape of the driveway was perfect for the zigzagging drunks who sauntered through.

Twenty marble steps welcomed us into the main floor, which was a story above the lawn. I learned how to count to twenty on those steps. "One, two, three, four, five, I can do it. Don't hold me, Yaya, I can do it. Six, seven, eight, nine, ten."

A woodworker carved on the main double doors a gold-plated relief of sinewy, thorny florae: plant carvings on the doors resembling the offerings in our gardens—birds-of-paradise, tropical orchids, bamboo, Indian mangoes—but spinier and barbed, as if they were about to hiss. The real plants, on the other hand, smelled fresh like a waterfall and didn't look so much like snakes. The mansion was like that—it housed many contradictions: my aristocratic mother and self-made father, our family's dependence on wealth and our helpers' faith, and many adults' agendas and my childhood dreams.

Inside the main doors, a gold-framed mirror the size of a small car hung over a console, where guests adjusted their ties and posture. My mother retouched her lipstick in front of it before leaving the house each morning.

In the grand ballroom, I played princess. It was the most spacious part of the mansion, a gold-plated square the same size and opulence as the historic Manila Hotel Centennial Hall. The walls sparkled in sand-colored stone, and the floor gleamed in an expanse of pearl-and-oyster marble, a mermaid's castle.

Stone terraces extended from the ballroom and the top floor. Bare of furniture and décor, the terrace was the ideal place for pondering the world outside. The terrace overlooked a fishpond and a rice paddy, where a farmer, along with his wife and sons, grew and harvested the Philippines' staple foods. I watched them from the terraces, wondering how and why they withstood the sun's heat.

"A young lady like you should never be out in the sun. Besides, you're already dark. Too dark. We have to keep you out of the sun or you'll look like those poor farmers," my mother would say. This was the same reason I never learned how to ride a bike. But when she wasn't home and the nannies were glued to the screen watching a telenovela, I walked out to the terrace and let the wind—which carried the little brown birds hovering over the paddy—blow my hair, whisk my skirt up, and sway me.

On the terrace, I heard the ancient church bells of the convent next door, where the nuns prayed the rosary and sang the Hail Mary in unison.

Hail Mary, full of grace. The Lord is with Thee. Blessed art Thou amongst women, and blessed is the fruit of Thy womb, Jesus. Holy Mary, Mother of God, pray for us sinners, now and at the hour of our death.

Then a full, long, resounding in-unison high contralto: *Aaaaaah-mmmehnnn.*

Papa adored their singing and rewarded them with regular rations of rice. Their hymns and invocations became my background music; they were the accompaniment to the stages of life in the mansion—the soundtrack to my preschool, grade school, and preteen years. The nuns created for me a holy atmosphere, a sheltering sound where I could

abide. Wherever I was, as long as I could hear them, I had somewhere
to hide.

My father made his money in the dining hall. He had an office,
yes, but that served as storage for typewriters, contracts, blueprints,
and ledgers. The real work took place where we ate, where he and his
kumpares feasted over coconut crab, lobster, and bouillabaisse. The oval
dining table seated at least twelve—where my father made eleven other
oil investors and manpower recruiters richer. Not that their houses in
Hong Kong, Dubai, and Singapore weren't large enough. The oil and
manpower-recruitment industries were stable and booming. The men
were merely bored. So when the Gulf War started, they were all shaken
off their thrones. The oval table had no corners for them to hold on to.

"What's a meal without a drink?" my parents would say. That's what
the bar was for. Not a trolley with an ice bucket, but our own taproom
playing Christopher Cross and Spandau Ballet. What my parents lacked
in musical knowledge, they made up for in their collection of beer,
wine, and Rémy Martin. I never told them, but my brother occasionally
stole San Miguel beer from the cooler. I, on the other hand, was always
good. I only asked the bartender for Shirley Temples. I drank them on
the barstool in my crinoline Marks & Spencer dress, my yaya holding
me so I wouldn't fall. She often gossiped to the bartender about our
family. Si Misis nanglalalake, si Ser wala nang pera. The missus cheats
on her husband; the mister has no more money. I always heard what
she said and, worse, I understood.

Next to the bar were two stairwells. The one on the left took you
to the two "extra" upstairs bedrooms. They were called "extra" because
the occupants changed as frequently as the monsoon brought rain
to the tropics. The first few years, they belonged to my yaya and her
sister, Judith. They were our nannies and were head of the house staff—
matronas, we called them. When they left, and my parents stopped
sleeping in the same bed, my father took over the tucked-away rooms.
He used one room for sleeping and the other to store the ruins of his

empire: yellowing sheets of contracts, dust-covered plaques, and photographs of him shaking hands with other suits-and-ties.

The stairwell on the right took you downstairs, where the help lived and where I often played. Downstairs was where I learned how to braid hair, how to skip rope, and how to eat balut—a common Southeast Asian street food: a developing duck embryo boiled alive in its shell. Downstairs was a whole other universe—one to which I wished I belonged.

Past the stairwells stood the breakfast room, where my mother seemed most serene and lovely to me. The light coming through the French doors filled the room with a whiteness, a cloud where I could catch and swallow dust sifting through beams. On a daily basis, the servants filled the breakfast room with floral arrangements as high and fragrant as my mother's hair. At our morning meal, Papa, Paolo, and I sat in white armchairs, while Mama sat in her favorite white rattan peacock chair. The maids stood against the wall in waiting, their clothes smelling like whatever had been tossed into the omelet du jour: onion, garlic, tomatoes, or Papa's and my favorite, corned beef from a can.

In the center of the house stood the disco, a rectangular marble space accessed from adjacent rooms through arched entryways. After drinks at the bar, my parents took their colleagues and friends into the glass-roofed atrium for a short sway to jazz tunes or a late-night samba or cha-cha. It was in that sparkly mirror-ball-lit room that my brother and I learned to, as he put it, "really get into the music." I tried to copy his dance moves—his isolations, gyrations, and the running man. I helped him put records on the turntable, pulling out the vinyl from their crisp sleeves.

The master bedroom took up the far corner of the main floor. It was the biggest bedroom in the house, and the only one with a walk-in closet, double vanity, his-and-her toilets, a bidet, a Jacuzzi, a built-in cosmetics organizer, two balconies, and its own well and garden. It had a king-size bed with built-in drawers, a davenport and chaise lounge, a coffee table, and two armchairs. It boasted a large TV equipped with both Betamax and VHS. The master bedroom had mood lighting and glowed in Louis Comfort Tiffany and capiz shell décor.

Right outside my parents' room, a door was camouflaged as part of the wall. This secret entrance led to the basement, which was my mother's closet. The basement housed her most prized possessions, her shopping compulsion and rituals: her shoes, jewelry, purses, and clothes. It was a private fashion exhibit containing as many stilettos as former First Lady Imelda Marcos's palace held. For a while, this was my favorite part of the house. It was a girl's playland. There I tried on my mother's Dior heels, twirled in her petticoat skirt, and played little brown Audrey Hepburn in her little black dress.

Every few weeks, our couturier, Mr. Albrando, measured and fitted us in his creations. On those days, merienda took place in the basement—coffee and Fita biscuits. In between sips and bites, Mama pointed out pictures in *Vogue* and *Elle*. "That one! Make me something just like that!" Mr. Albrando obliged and always overcomplimented, in his made-up accent that was a cross between Old Castilian Money and British, "Of course, of course! Oh, Madam Doctora, you will look so good in that—better than that model!" But his accent was fake and his clothes made me uncomfortable. I asked our yaya, "How can someone not know that ruffled lace makes you itch?"

Where the secret closet door ended, the long dark hallway began. Our "boys," our male servants, did everything to light up that corridor: recessed lighting, suspended spotlights, floor lamps, sconces, even electric torches. They all eventually sparked, blew, and died. The house staff—whom my mother called "ignorant and superstitious"—believed that dark spirits roamed the hall. I believed it, too.

The hallway's length varied over the years. The older I got, the longer it seemed to be. What started out as a span of twelve toddler steps later on stretched to a thirteen-meter dash, a sprint, a chase to the finish line for my dear life.

I never want to walk down that hallway again.

The last room on the main floor sat at the front part of the mansion. We called that room the lanai, which means "roofed patio." It's not the kind of patio that wraps around colonial houses, nor is it a fire-pit area. It was half indoors, half outdoors, always smelling like moss and artificially ventilated air. It felt dry on sunny days and wet when it rained. Papa liked to have his beer and boiled peanuts there. Mama rarely visited. "Too humid," she said when it rained. "Too hot," she said when the sun blazed. Papa called the lanai "part forest, part desert," his home within our home from where he and I watched the sky.

The main floor ended where another world began: the stairs to the top floor. The stairs backed up against a twelve-meter, two-story-high window. The window flooded the steps and upstairs corridors with natural light. Standing there, I felt very close to heaven.

Four bedrooms made up the highest section of the house: the guest room, my brother's teenage bedroom, my bedroom, and my brother's room that he'd had when he was a child. I considered it to be the most peaceful part of the house. There we kept books, sketch pads, crayons, dolls, giant stuffed animals, Matchbox cars, Game Boys, Nintendo consoles, and our favorite blankets. It was where Paolo and I pretended to be pilots, presidents, fairies, Mom, Dad, and peasant child.

I slept in a princess bed with carved wood columns that held up an eyelet-cotton canopy. Most of my toys were kept in a glass cabinet over my dresser, where dust could not touch them. The dresser held a broad mirror in which I later saw the flaws my mother pointed out: my dark morena skin, my flat nose, my round belly and flabby arms, and my big beaver teeth. The same dresser kept gold chain necklaces, earrings, and pearl bracelets my Saudi Arabian godfathers gifted me.

On the top floor, my brother and I laughed and played and ran and cried and screamed—and nobody on the main floor or downstairs could hear us. It was our very own island.

A puzzle of diamond-shaped mirrors covered the mansion's ceiling, and where their tips met, crystal chandeliers hung. They sparkled so much, I couldn't resist plucking them out. I stacked footrests on top of chairs and chairs on top of tables, and climbed up my makeshift ladder ever so lithely, gazing to the top with twinkling eyes, my big beaver teeth biting into my lower lip. The sparkly glass puzzle that hovered above resembled a kaleidoscope—a prism of rainbows and reflections, of pieces cutting through patterns, shifting and rotating, mirroring the jumble, the circus, and the wonder within. I was a little girl who loved to twirl, often in a polka-dot petticoat skirt—my mother's purchase and my father's delight. After I had plucked my crystal and descended from the tower of furniture, I twirled, with a chandelier trinket secured in my hand. I twirled, looking up to my illusion of a Technicolor sky. I twirled, dizzying and dizzying.

Falling.

PART ONE

Garden Party

I was born two pounds small with a diamond-shaped birthmark on my left palm. A contradiction, a paradox of holy signs, my yaya and the maids had said. The common masses, which my mother spoke about with a raised brow, believed that the birthmark meant good luck for business. The dark brown smear at the axis of my palm's fate and heart lines heralded fortune after fortune for Papa's ventures. The diamond, which looked like a distant star in mid-twinkle, projected my parents' professional plans and encouraged them to sign on every deal.

"My Lucky Star," Papa called it, rubbing and kissing my hand as if it belonged to Our Lady of Good Fortune, or better yet, a shiny Golden Buddha gifted by a Taiwanese investor.

But the maids also pointed out that the star was on my left palm—the bad palm, the "other" hand, Satan's preferred side. Kaliwete.

And my premature birth, others thought, was the evidence of sin. "Whose sin?" the maids speculated. It gave gossip hour something straight out of their beloved, melodramatic teleseryes. Was it the sin of my father? Was it evidence of his not having legally terminated his first marriage—the marriage he was forced into at age seventeen? Or was it evidence of my parents' fake nuptials—the falsified certificates, the joint bank accounts opened as the consummation of their union, the thousand glittery, champagne-toasted parties in lieu of a wedding reception?

Or was it the sin of my mother? Was it atonement for the many previous pregnancies intentionally or unintentionally terminated? Was the Catholic Church right after all, that every pregnancy was a life, and every life was worth a mother's time on bed rest, no matter how busy or affluent or important she was? Or was my early birth a resurfacing of Mama's long-kept, deeply buried secret, one that Paolo and I suspected every time she called me by another name: Mara, meaning bitter. Was my coming in haste "from heaven to earth," as Papa used to say, punishment for having dishonestly baptized Paolo as Mama's firstborn? Was my rash arrival an ejection from the womb—a utero-muscular reaction to the lullabies she hummed to a chestful of baby-girl clothes that were never mine?

My coming was the beginning of what the maids referred to as sira-ulo—broken head. Over the years, Mama repeatedly lamented the moments of the day I was born. She appealed to an imaginary court.

"Those doctors were incompetent! I would have had you full-term had they just left me at my office instead of rushing me to the ER. I wasn't overworked. They need to stop blaming my duties and my parties and my heels. There was absolutely no need for an emergency induction or meds or IVs. I was fine. You were fine. It was supposed to be fine."

Papa always answered with his typical optimism. He focused on how well I made it through months of being in an incubator—a plastic womb—and how quickly I fattened up, how the tubes sticking into my nose, belly button, and arms never kept me from learning how to coo and smile. He focused on my Lucky Star.

"She holds the sign of a good future ahead of us," Papa said sporadically, no matter the topic of conversation. "She is made of light, and so the star twinkles in her left hand."

Papa always pointed to the stars at night, the Manila sky as his favorite movie and Orion's belt as his favorite scene.

"That's Orion's belt, the most noticeable constellation. Those three stars always point to the North Star—that's you, Paolo, and me. Us three, always pointing to our true north, always looking to the light. Alnitak, Alnilam, Mintaka. These stars will be with you always, especially in the dark of night. They were with me in the desert; they will be with you here. Always remember: We were not made for normal. And for that, I am sorry."

Was he wise? Or was he ignorant and superstitious? Was I a wound, a scar—stigmata impressed upon the skin by sin? Was I born of flesh or was I born of light?

Papa once read to me from a children's encyclopedia: "Supernovas shine their brightest when they explode and die."

1989

My parents should have thrown me a birthday party with balloons or clowns or puppeteers, and party hats and sprinkles and a piñata. Instead, they lavished me with three ball gowns for the day, a tower of champagne glasses sparkling in the hot sun, an emcee paid to announce the arrival of VIPs, and an octagon table the size of a bed for the guests' largesse: tins of Turkish delight, matching gold bracelets and necklaces, velvet hair bows bigger than my head, and oddly, the most age-appropriate of them all, Rollerblade Barbie with lighters for skates. The long-legged doll was a gift from a young woman and a young man who referred to themselves as my half sister and half brother.

"You don't really know us," they said, "but we have the same father."

The young man showed me how to make Barbie's skates flicker. The skates sparked a small flame when they skidded against the floor. I was both delighted by that Barbie and scared of it. Little rich Filipino girls didn't often play with fire, or any of the other elements: air, water, or soil. We were kept clean and unsweaty by our yayas, our nannies. But really, my parents should've let me get sweaty, let me eat cotton candy, let me get frosting on my clothes, dirt under my toenails, and silly string in my hair. They should've given me that kid-themed party, what would've been my third, because it was also to be my last.

I was never to have a birthday party again.

The mansion would not have another reason to celebrate.

Most guests at the party didn't know who I was and had never talked to me, but it didn't bother me because I was too busy stealing licks of icing from the back side of the garden-themed cake. I was too busy ripping lace ruffles off the socks that made my ankles itch. My yaya caught me behind the three-tiered cake, licking fondant roses, and with a handful of lace shreds, and hoisted me back up to my room for a scrub-down of my face or a change of itchy socks to even itchier socks. Or worse, for an Aqua Net spray spree, making my slick hair stiff as bamboo.

Paolo, my mother's son from her first marriage, spent the entirety of the party at the DJ booth, watching how vinyl was spun and scratched to make Michael Jackson or Madonna sound like Prince or Boy George.

Copying my brother's dance moves was the most fun part for me: how he stuck his elbows out and followed this move with a pop of the shoulders and a snap, also known as the love shack; or how he did the MC Hammer—a fluid squiggle of his limbs and an abrupt lock, followed by a squat, a jump, and landing on a crisscrossed stance; or the best one, the one I couldn't emulate—the magical gliding backward across the floor, the then-ubiquitous moonwalk.

"Not like that, like this," my brother said, showing me how to properly isolate my neck and limbs from my torso. His constant correcting, teaching, and mocking were his way of reminding me that he was five years older than I was.

"I'm try*ing*, Kuya. Look," I said, spasming to the beat.

"Whatever, get away from me," he said.

"It's my birthday and Mama had the garden decorated for me!" I said with arms crossed.

"Yeah, yeah. Whatever you say. For you, all for you."

"Do you not like it?"

"Do you?"

I shrugged.

I can't remember blowing out candles on my cake. In fact, I will have no memories of ever blowing out birthday candles. It will be one of those things that I remembered from other kids' parties, but never experienced myself. Mama believed that what was more important were the outfits and the fondant roses and the red carpet strewn down the main staircase and the patent leather shoes and the purple orchids and the polished jade urns and the sheen on the mirrors and the fresh shellfish and the restaurant-grade crabmeat. "I love you and I want the best for you," she always said. And to her, love was as big as the rocks on her ring and earrings, as wide as the garden that accommodated her guests, and as deep as the blue blood that ran in her veins.

But I recall linking arms with my brother for the champagne toast. It was one of our few family traditions—to toast to the celebrant's good health and good future, in medicine or the oil business, and to sip champagne, arms braided with your closest confidant. I didn't have champagne, of course. I had bittersweet apple cider in a flute.

"Better a flute than that damn baby bottle," Mama said. She made sure that the yaya hid my bottle, which I'd drunk from since the day I was discharged from the neonatal unit.

My brother, however, took sips of alcohol whenever my parents brought out an import or a vintage from their collection. They let him, and he loved it—one sip here, a swig there.

If not caught in conversation with Mama and her peers, Papa carried me around and introduced me to his friends and colleagues. He kissed my cheek and my Lucky Star after every time he said, "This is my youngest. My darling girl. I can't believe she's three." His guests

replied with a tip of their glass, and if Catholic, with a sign of the
cross thumbed on my forehead. If Arab, like most of Papa's oil friends,
they replied with as-salaam alaikum and a firm handshake. I didn't
like their handshakes because I didn't like their hands. Men's hands
frightened me.

Mama walked up and down our driveway in heels, where the buffet
and gift tables were set up and where the drunken guests drifted. She
was twenty-six weeks pregnant, and although her belly barely showed,
her ankles were plump like ripe mangoes. Her empire-waist bouffant
dress came down to mid-shin, emphasizing her bulging shanks. The
tight velveteen bow around her waist cinched her in half.

"Half pregnant, half in denial," the maids whispered. "Parang si
Sisa." Like Sisa, the Filipino literary character we all knew as the crazy
one.

The maids always made fun of Mama's ridiculous outfits—how she
wore black Chanel blazers in the hot tropic sun, or how she coiffed her
hair in flowers taller than the dining room centerpiece. While Mama
occupied herself with besos, the maids joked about her and her ornately
dressed amigas from behind the buffet or kitchen table.

As my parents entertained their investors, they left me in the company of the maids: Angge and Judith—who only *I* knew were lovers;
my yaya Lorna; Dehlia; Masing; Loring; and the youngest one at only
fourteen, Katring. I spent most of my time at home with them, hearing
everything they had to say. They gossiped about my family in Tagalog.

"Did you see that one madam? Her clothes were so tight, she
couldn't breathe," one of them said.

"What about the other one, the really skinny one? The one that
goes to the gym with Doctora?" another said.

"Does that one even eat? Too skinny. Maybe she lost so much
weight because her daughter was kidnapped."

"Uck. Poor girl. The syndicate scooped her eye out with a spoon!"

"Well, when you flaunt your wealth as if it were the Feast of the Blessed Child Jesus, that's what you get! Kidnappers scooping out your kid's eye! Hay naku!"

Hahahahaha.

Downstairs, they cackled their hearts out about the people partying on the main floor. And I did, too.

Everyone had gone. The yayas had given me and Paolo our evening bath—we took two every day—and they combed our hair while we watched *Teenage Mutant Ninja Turtles*. One hundred brushstrokes a night, Mama ordered, no more or no less. My hair was wet and flat and felt cold against my neck and back. The hairbrush bristles rubbed my scalp raw; how well they knew my sensitive spots. It gave me goose bumps on my arms and a *ting* on the lobes of my ears.

"Yaya, where are Mama and Papa?" I said.

"Hospital," she said, matter-of-factly, still brushing my hair.

"What? Why?" I said.

"Because Mama's giving birth, Batchoy," Paolo said.

"What? But it's *my* birthday. Papa said the baby would come during rainy season."

"Mama started getting tummy aches, so they took her, okay? Now, shh!"

"But it's *my* birthday," I said. "Mine, mine, mine."

"You're going to cry because you're not the baby anymore?" Paolo said. "And because now you and the baby will share a birthday? Boo-ya. Get over it."

I sobbed until the show was over, protesting to my yaya against sharing my birthday with another kid. She pulled out my bottle from the dresser's top drawer, tucked me into bed, and lay next to me, patting me on the thigh to help me fall asleep, as she always did. She patted rhythmically and just as slowly as I needed her to and quelled my panic to hiccupy breathing. She stroked my hair and whispered to me that the baby and I were born in different years, which technically meant we didn't have the same birthday. She said we could have separate birthday parties in the future—mine in the garden and the baby's in the ballroom, and if I chose to share a party, we could still have two separate cakes. She also said that I was *exactly* three years older, which was a really big deal—I could use it against her, or him. "I'm three years older, so you have to follow me, little one," I practiced saying while I fell asleep. "Three years. That means I'm bigger than you, little one. Three big years."

"Now say your prayers and say good night," Yaya said, as she patted me to sleep.

I teethed on and sucked the rubber nipple on my baby bottle, mumbling from the corner of my mouth, "Thank you, God, for everything. Good night, fan. Good night, lamp. Good night, bed. Good night, toys. Good night, moon. Good night, Yaya. Good night, Paolo. Good night, baby in Mama's belly. Good night, mansion."

I was three years and half-a-night old when Paolo woke me up. He stood next to my bed, holding my arm and shaking it.

"Wake up, Batchoy," he said with a soft, scratchy voice. Then he took my hand, which he never did, pulled me up, and wiped a tear from his cheek.

"Where are we going?" I said, rubbing my eyes. "Are you crying, Kuya?"

"Mama and Papa want to talk to us and show us something," he said, sniffing.

By how tightly he held my hand and how his shoulders slumped, I knew it wasn't the time to be asking too many questions. My right hand clung to Paolo's, while my left held the baby bottle.

We walked together from my room to the stairs.

The mansion was dark, except for the moonlight coming through the twelve-meter staircase window. It was quiet, with only soft sniffs echoing through the long dark hallway and up to our floor. With every step down, the sniffs became louder and more familiar—they were Mama's. She walked toward us, and we followed the sound. Papa trailed closely behind her, not rushing to give me a kiss or a hug. We met at the foot of the stairs: a family of not four, but five. A little one cradled in Mama's shaking arms.

"Ang kapatid niyo." Your brother, Papa said in Tagalog, which he never used around us or Mama or anybody else from our class. "Eto ang kapatid niyo, pero nasa langit na siya." Here's your brother, but he's in heaven now.

I loved him when I saw him, even though he was already a little heap of cold blue flesh. If love was the feeling you got every time your dad walked through the door after a business trip, or if love was the snugness you felt in your chest every time you saw your parents dance together and laugh. I loved him when I saw him, and my love for him made it hard to talk or breathe or swallow, even though I didn't quite understand why he was in heaven—why he didn't stay long enough to meet us. Maybe my whining about our shared birthday scared him away. My yaya did say one time that children were very intuitive, that they always knew what you were thinking, no matter how hard you tried to lie. I guess I was intuitive like him, too. I loved him, I just knew.

Mama said nothing until we put the baby in the box.

"Wait!" she said, clutching him like a football. "Not yet. Let's give him a name."

"What should we call him?" Papa said.

"Name him after the food I craved while I was pregnant. Pistachio nuts."

"Pistachio? Are you sure?" Papa said, asking without protesting.

"Yes. We'll call him Tachio."

I thought it was perfect, a name derived from a little wrinkly nut that was green but pale. Just like he was—small and puckered wherever his blood had gone. His body balled up in the white cotton swaddle like a pistachio in its shell.

"Tachio," Paolo and I whispered together with pleased grins.

"Tachio, my sweet boy," Papa said with a sigh as he took the baby from Mama's arms. He kissed his forehead and placed him in a wooden coffin no bigger than a shoe box. It was then that Mama wailed, her chest expanding and collapsing, expanding and collapsing, until she fell on her knees to where the moonlight met the floor. Paolo and I had never seen Mama act that way; she was always put-together and poised. We didn't move or hug her or hold her hand. We didn't know what to do. So he and I both turned to our yayas and buried our faces in their stomachs, wetting their shirts with tears.

Papa walked us to the main door and down the grand staircase still draped with a red velvet carpet. Décor from my birthday festivities had not yet been put away. A trail of confetti led us through the garden and to the grotto, where our three-meter sculpture of Our Lady of Peace and Good Voyage stood. She was a sky-blue-cloaked saint with a golden halo for a crown, holding the Baby Jesus in her porcelain-smooth hands. Mestiza, like Mama and Tachio—fair skin, raised nose bridge, thin lips, round doe-shaped eyes. Mestiza, unlike me, Paolo, and Papa. Our Lady stood on a man-made hill at the far corner of the garden, overlooking the highway, the mansion, the convent, and the pond. My parents chose to bury Tachio at the foot of the hill, within arm's reach of Our Lady, where a mestiza—her sacred power encased in white Castilian skin— could watch over him. We stood in front of that hill as if it were an altar, a consecrated knoll displaying the colonizer's gifts to the bloodline: Christianity, education, and rank.

The male servants had been digging a hole for my brother's coffin. Once we got to the site, Papa took over and dug some more. He didn't cry, but he dug intently and made a hole large enough for him and my baby brother. When he'd finally used up all his strength, Papa called me and Paolo over to say a prayer and one last goodbye. He told us we could kiss Tachio on the cheek if we wanted to, so we did.

"Be a good boy, Tachio. We love you," Paolo said.

"Yeah, be a good boy, Tachio. We love you," I said.

"Stop copying me," Paolo said.

I furrowed my brows and stuck my tongue out at him. Then I turned back to Tachio and gave him my bottle.

"So you won't be hungry in heaven," I said.

My parents and Yaya had been coaxing and coaching me away from the bottle and toward using a cup for two years. They'd tried every trick and method. And that night, in the garden full of oriental flowers, tropical fruit trees, champagne glasses, and a dead baby, I finally weaned.

Orchids in the Morning

1990

Mama was soft at breakfast. Soft like the orange on her plate, like the ripples from where the tea bag met the hot water in her cup. Soft like the curves of her teaspoon and the collar of her robe; supple like the palms of her well-moisturized hands. She was as pure and easy as morning's air. And I breathed her in.

She was such a lady, more than any other time, when she sat down and dillydallied over a magazine, leafing, almost combing through it, as if it were the hair of her lost child. It was in the breakfast room where my mother seemed most lucid and lovely to me. Maybe it was the yellow-white morning light coming through the French doors, or the pinkness on her cheeks reflected from the terra-cotta floor, or the orchids she picked from the last well-kept garden in the house.

Or maybe it was the fact that she was there at dayspring—her best hour. She was a morning person; the rest of us were not.

Papa didn't show up at breakfast awake or ready. He was there to yawn, stretch, and have coffee, to lean into his sleepiness one last time before giving in to the demands of the day. Mama, however, was there to be there—as if breakfast were an affair for invited guests and not the preparations that came before, as if all happiness depended on a leisurely first meal.

When Mama stalled, the maids hurried. They hurried to get Paolo and me into our school uniforms. But we didn't want to get dressed. A shoe was kicked off the foot three times before it was tied. I refused to let my tangled black hair be combed. I shrieked every time my yaya brushed it. I picked at my socks because the lace around them was itchy. I pouted and squirmed and refused to eat my breakfast. I made clicking sounds with my tongue. I made faces at Paolo.

"Malikot," Yaya would say. A word that meant both "restless" and "playful." A notion of both acceptance and annoyance.

"Hmph," I would say back, with arms crossed at my chest and brows puckered in a frown. Then I would look up and catch Papa looking at me, not through the glasses balancing on his nose but over them and the top of the newspaper he was reading. He gave me the look that sweet-tempered fathers give their daughters when they've done something wrong, pulling his lower lip over his top teeth and gazing at me with unhappy, but not angry, eyes. I knew what he meant. He wanted me to stop, be still, and watch my mother. He wanted me to pause and catch it in its rareness.

So I watched.

Mama browsed issues of *Vogue*, *Elle*, and *Panorama*. She licked her finger before turning the page and studied every picture as if it were a work of art. She whispered *hmm* every time she saw something she adored—a dress, a hat, a pair of shoes—dog-earing the pages and coming back to them to rip them out, then placing them in a folder, along with other ensembles she'd found inspiring.

Then Mama looked up at me and Paolo and asked, "You want to pick your favorite outfits, too?"

Paolo and I nodded, very quickly, as if the offer could be taken away. We walked around to the top of the table where Mama's white rattan peacock chair stood. He and I each sat on an armrest, feeling

Mama's warmth, yet not touching her body. She brought the magazine closer and flipped through, stopping wherever Paolo and I saw something we liked.

"That one with her shoulders showing," I said. "I like her top."

"What do you like about it?" Mama asked.

"I like that it's black."

"Black is always a good color. Elegant and effortless." She smiled at me and tucked my outgrown bangs behind my ear, then asked the maid to fetch a few more folders from the office, wrote our names on them, and said, "These are your folders. Your collections."

She called out words—words that she thought we could add to our vocabulary.

"Cordial!" she said out loud, looking up, then back down to read.

"Affluent!"

"Recherché!"

"Prêt-à-porter!"

That made Papa smile. There was very little they agreed on, but the silliness and spontaneity involved in spitting out words to the morning air must have rekindled his affections for her. I needed it to. When I watched him watch her at breakfast, I could almost understand what he loved about her in the first place. She was smart, stylish, and pretty. She knew her fashion as well as she knew her dictionary. She was everything every Filipino wanted to be—fluent in the languages of Europe and the Americas, clothed in imports, and with passports stamped in Arabic, Chinese, and English. The things she loved, she loved much, and she was completely given over to them: the designer clothes, the academic achievements, the mansion, the connections, and the political ties.

At breakfast, Mama didn't talk about other people—not her aerobics friends, her cocktail party friends, her doctor friends, nor her sisters. Instead she talked about my hair, how pretty it was when it was up in a bun, and how it accentuated my jaw and forehead, the very facial features I got from her. She also talked about my cheekbones—which

I got from Papa—how they were high but friendly, and how on them a kind smile could hang.

She talked about her orchids—deep purple whorls of globular petals—how they were her "most favorite thing in the world." She described them as regal, graceful, delicate, and rare. She called them "exotic" and explained that the orchid's purpose was purely ornamental. She argued, "I don't agree with the Greeks that orchids are for fertility. If that were true, I'd have a garden full of babies."

I thought she was right. Every time I got a whiff of the orchid's perfume, I smelled exactly what she described—something poised, something tropical, something striking and sure of its draw. I confused that smell with the scent my mother wore, Anaïs Anaïs by Cacharel.

In between sipping tea and eating an orange, Mama hummed the tune from our Betamax tape rewinder. She hummed it with amusement, like she was humming a song sung by Julie Andrews, and not a cheap tune played by an electronic plastic square. She wasn't a singer, but her singing with closed lips comforted me. It was hard to believe that from those same lips came yesterday's wounding words: "Stop playing in the sun! You're already dark, too dark! Like a maid!"

Mama talked about what Paolo and I were like as babies. She emphasized how small I was—two pounds exactly at birth. She talked about how much she hated not being able to take me home, and how some people were just "plain insensitive" because they kept referring to me as a mouse. She said that she paid for the best incubators the hospital could find and insisted that I had no reason to ever fear.

"You've been through so much, yet you were so little. You've been through the worst of it, and you fought for your life. You can handle anything. Those doctors said you'd never make it, but here you are, eating breakfast with me. I kept you alive."

Then Mama's temper started to get heated and her tone changed from calm to controlled. She brought her teacup and saucer up to her mouth and held them there, not sipping—just supporting them from the base and handle. The lusterware trembled with her manicured hands. Her cup and saucer clinked in rhythm with my heartbeat. I opened my mouth into a little O, inhaling, drinking what could be the morning's last dewdrop of Mama's softness.

She set down her cup and breakfast ended.

There was no lingering of any kind. The chinking of silverware stopped. The chairs were pushed back and then in and under the table. Magazines were left open to the last page read. Forks and spoons (not knives—those were for dinner) left the proper way, at the two o'clock position. When breakfast ended, there was no orange left on Mama's plate, just the peel.

When Mama got up, I got up. I followed her to her bedroom, into her makeup room, trailing so close behind her as if to catch the tail end of her softness. As soon as we walked into that room filled with palette after palette of makeup, I knew it was gone. It was no longer Breakfast Mama I was standing next to. It was Mama made of cosmetics from Rustan's, Manila's upscale department store.

Getting Dressed Mama was keen and swift, like the wind that blew a door shut. She walked over to her clothes valet like a lioness with eyes fixed on her prey—a pressed wrap dress or blazer in zebra, cheetah, or leopard print. She sat her five-foot-flat figure on her upholstered vanity stool. And there began the transformation—from au naturel to clad.

"Come watch," she said, dabbing a wedge sponge on a pot of foundation, then priming one side of her face with it. She handed me the sponge and told me to try it.

"Like this?" I said, touching her face so gently that the motion left little to no effect on her skin.

"No, dab it like you mean it. Cover the blemishes on my face. Like this one right here," she said.

I looked at her, not at the mirror, and saw none.

"Okay," I said, smearing yellowish-beige product from her temple to her chin.

She walked me through the different strokes of applying makeup, teaching me tricks for an angled contour, shading and blending. She taught me the layers of an "original glow"—moisturizer, primer, foundation, concealer, blush, and bronzer.

"Now take this," she said, handing me a brow brush she'd dipped in orchid-purple eye shadow.

When she felt like I was ready, she gave me permission to do her eyes, that is, to make them look bigger and deeper set. I learned how to turn a mono eyelid into a perfectly creased almond shape; a dark shade on the outer corner of the eye turned it into something very mestiza.

Mama showed me how to curl and volumize stubborn Filipina lashes. She used a blow-dryer to heat a lash curler and crimped the short hairs with it. Then she finished them with several coats of mascara. She outlined her brows with a brown-black pencil, making her face sharp and strong.

Next she did her lips. She traced them with a maroon stick, then spread rouge from the inside to the corners of the upper lip, and twice from side to side on the lower. She pressed her lips onto tissue to seal the color in her puckers. Her lips were so red, so pronounced, that I could focus on nothing else in the room; it was a scarlet that outclassed everything around it.

Then her robe came off. She untied the sash, and the silk cover-up fell from her shoulders, sliding off her arms and onto the floor. The maids picked up the robe later, long after she'd left the room and was at lunch or a meeting.

The maids ushered me away from the makeup room and to the chaise lounge, where her selection of Hermès bags sat, to brush my hair as I looked at and longed for Mama, who was three meters away.

Getting dressed was not something I could help with. Mama made it her business and nobody else's. It was a rite she took pride in, basked in, and savored. As she and Papa drifted apart, she had her clothes and the time it took to put them on to hold on to.

When the clothes were on, she slid her feet into designer heels. She owned a collection of over one hundred pairs, every Christian Dior style in every color. She was a few pairs away from dethroning Imelda Marcos as Queen of Shoes. When she wore her red pumps, I imagined her as grown-up Dorothy from *The Wizard of Oz*, but in my mind, she said, "Toto, we're not in Manila anymore. We're somewhere better: *My*-nila."

When the shoulder pads were fixed, and the stray hair was bobby-pinned and glued down with Aqua Net, there was one last thing to do: Spray on Anaïs Anaïs perfume. She spritzed twice on her wrists, twice on the neck, and once in the air for her to walk through. That was the crowning moment, the scent of bottled orchid.

Mama turned to me, then to the mirror, then to me again. She placed her hands on her hips, raised her chin, and smiled the smile she used for the press, and said, "There."

Falling

1990

Minutes after she sat down for dinner, Mama began uttering phrases that made Papa slump in his seat and made Lorna and Judith cover Paolo's and my ears. "You all brought bad luck into my life. Putang ina kayong lahat."

After her litany, Mama grabbed a carafe by the neck, held it up an arm's length away from her side, and let go of it, saying, "Everything is falling."

She then pushed back her chair, got up, and stormed off to her basement closet, calling out words to the evening air and expanding our vocabulary and fright. "Descend! Dive! Plummet! Plunge! Topple! Tumble! Stumble! Subside! Dwindle! Diminish! *Die.*" She locked herself in her closet and found solace in shelves full of designer friends: Christian, Louis, Salvatore, and Coco.

Papa stood up and walked around to our side of the table, patted Paolo's head, and bent down to kiss my cheek. He told Angge to sweep up and took his beer and paper to the lanai, knowing that Mama never set foot in the muggy room. Broken pieces of glass sparkled on the marble floor. Beads of lemon iced tea seeped into the weaving of Mama's rattan chair. Lorna picked up our plates and instructed us to go upstairs and said that we could finish supper while watching a show.

Once upstairs, Paolo and I had no interest in eating. Instead, we played. He turned on his Nintendo console and put on Janet Jackson's *Rhythm Nation*. I played house and pretended to be taking care of Tachio: feeding him and bathing him and rocking and singing him to sleep.

"Shhh, night-night, little one. Close your eyes. Shhhhh. Happy birthday to you. Happy birthday to me. Happy birthday to brother and sister. Happy birthday, you and me."

I talked to him about how he got his name, how Mama ate pistachio nuts every day that she was pregnant with him, how she preferred his nose and lips and skin over mine. I told him that he could use anything that I owned—my toys were his toys because we shared a birthday.

I turned four that deathly hot Philippine summer, and Tachio would've turned one. I knew that he grew a year older every time I did, but he was always the same baby to me—a few hours old, mestizo, and dead cold. That was exactly what I pictured him to be when I played pretend. It frightened the household staff when they asked me with whom I was chuckling in my room.

"Neng." Katring called me by the lower-class diminutive version of my name. "Who are you playing with?"

"Si Tachio," I said, cradling a bundle of sheets in my arms.

"Hoy! Don't play like that! Your brother might come back from the dead!" Angge said as the rest shuffled away in fear and marked the sign of the cross on their foreheads and hearts.

"But he's my toy *and* my friend," I said.

Then I whispered to the bundle of sheets, "It's okay. They're just stupid, like Mama says. We are not stupid, she says. We're like Lolo."

His imaginary face with the perfect nose and perfect lips eased up, and his imaginary crying stopped, and his imaginary doe-shaped eyes closed. He fell asleep in my embrace, cuddled in the warmth between a brother and his sister.

Unlike Tachio, Paolo and I grew and changed.

I grew fatter with each meal, as the maids followed Mama's orders to keep me well fed. Tachio and I had both been born premature, eight weeks shy of our due dates, and were born weighing less than three pounds. Same birthday, same size, same undernourished bodies. The difference was that I lived and he died. His death reminded Mama that children who were too small, too frail, could slip away from life. She had the maids feed me rice and noodles and starchy fruits, and they gave me hot Milo and Yakult cultured milk at least six times a day. It contradicted Mama's no-carb, no-salt, no-real-meals diet. Whatever she suffered not to eat, I gobbled down and deposited into my pan de sal thighs and jamon de bola belly.

I didn't complain. I didn't know how to. I didn't know to make the connection between the size of my thighs and the speed, or lack thereof, of my feet. I didn't know that when Paolo and his friends played tag in the garden, they always called me It because they knew I could never catch up. They knew I wasn't a runner. They knew that I would soon shy away from their games, leave them be, and walk upstairs to my bed to read, sketch, and play pretend.

"Napabayaan sa kusina!" Like she was left alone in the kitchen! was a common joke with Paolo and his pals. They said it often and with the heckling tone that belonged only to big brothers.

"Napabayaan sa kusina!" Paolo said, rolling off his chair, clutching at his stomach, and dying from laughter.

"Stop!" I said.

"Napabayaan sa kusina!" he said once more after getting back on his seat.

"I said stop! I'm telling Mama!" I said.

"I don't care. You're fat. I don't care."

"You used to be fat, too!"

"But I play soccer now. And you, you're just here playing with your pretend babies and talking to ghosts and coloring and reading and fat-fatfat!" he said, sticking his tongue out.

"Yaya! Yayaaaa!" I said, beginning to cry.

"Paolo, stop it now," Lorna said.

"Bleh. Yaya ka lang." You're just a nanny.

There was no winning against Paolo. My yaya said that he was a bully because he never got to spend time with his real father.

"He's just lucky your papa loves him like his own son," she said.

She took me upstairs, played a Betamax movie, and sat me in my plush bed. She fetched a tray of biscuits and rice cakes, and fed me again and again. And again.

Paolo changed the way all nine-year-old boys did. He became sweatier, stickier, taller, leaner, and meaner. While I was asleep, he struck silver forks against each other to make that scratchy, metallic sound that hurt the inside of my ears and the back of my mouth. He kept telling me that I had no shot at becoming a Ninja Turtle, especially not Donatello, because I wasn't street-smart or ninja enough. He knocked down my Lego towers right before I could top them off with the last block. He hid my dolls. He ate my candy. And he never ever—not in a bajillion-gazillion galactic years—let me play with his Game Boy.

It was the first half of 1990 and Papa and Mama were rarely home.

Paolo reported the headlines to our yayas, pretending to be a news anchor and holding a Pringles can at chest level—his microphone.

"Mikhail Gorbachev becomes president of the USSR. Michael Jordan averages sixty points per game. MC Hammer tops the charts with 'U Can't Touch This.' Imelda Marcos appears in court. And Arsenio Hall is *TV Guide*'s Personality of the Year."

Paolo read these facts out loud repeatedly, from the television screen and from covers and pages of glossies from the duty-free American store, to which our tutor would say, as if she weren't in the company of children under ten, "Ayayay! The new decade is all about politics, superstardom, sex, money, sex, money, money, sex, and fame."

My parents' lives were much the same.

Papa frequented Taiwan, Hong Kong, Singapore, New Zealand, Abu Dhabi, and the United States. He made deals with hotshots in the Arab world on oil and car-part imports to and exports from the archipelago, and deals with those hotshots' fathers and brothers to recruit Filipino men and women for blue-collar jobs. He met with elite Chinese businessmen—the kind who played golf and stayed at the Mandarin Oriental, and, like us, spoke perfect West Coast English—for trades.

"I give them something they want; they give me something I need," my father tried to teach us. "It's simple, it's business."

Mama ruled on the other end of the machine. She was a doctor, among many other things, and could approve a working-class man's work permit based on health. Papa found them jobs, and Mama checked them for TB and STDs, and charged the OFWs—overseas Filipino workers—a fixed fee for their services. People needed work and they paid my parents to get it. Papa said that it was a genius plan for the '90s—the decade of climbing the ranks and living life in full color.

Until the midyear crises struck.

As our televisions announced and blared, hundreds of people died in an earthquake in the northern mountains of the Philippines. Mama lost a few distant relatives and childhood friends, but was only fazed by their deaths for a day. A few weeks later, on August 7, 1990, Papa and Mama shook their heads and *tsk-tsk*ed in front of the television when the news anchor said that the United States was to join the coalition against Iraq.

"Anak ng puta," both my parents said. "Anak ng puta yang si Saddam." Son of a bitch, that Saddam.

The Gulf War began.

Papa repeated the anchor's words for days, saying them under his breath and sweating, "Saddam. Naku. Diyos ko, huwag po. Not my men, please. Spare them. Not my men."

My parents' recruited laborers were displaced and dispersed throughout the Muslim-Arab world, caught in war zones, and Papa and Mama had to retrieve them, by all means, dead or alive, Papa explained to Mama. He rolled out a map of the world on the breakfast table and drew a red circle around the Middle East. He marked Xs where his men had likely scattered: Kuwait, Riyadh, Doha, Al Wakrah, Jeddah, and Abu Dhabi. He had Paolo bring him his plastic toy soldiers, which he positioned throughout the map—representations of where American troops were likely stationed or had attacked. Papa said that they had to pay countless officials, airlines, agencies, and civilians for repatriation. And he warned Mama that the mission to get everyone back would cost us tens of millions—my father's FossilFil Project alone had ten thousand Filipino workers.

"Thousands of workers," Papa said. "Good god."

"Meaning what, Gonzalo?" Mama said.

"Search and rescue, repatriation, flights, agencies, compensation for families of those who don't make it back, buying back their stash of Arab money, damage control."

"Well, fuckin' do something about it, Gonzalo," Mama demanded. "You cannot—*cannot*—let us drown."

Persian Gulf War. Operation Desert Storm. Operation Granby. First Gulf War. Liberation of Kuwait. Mother of All Battles. Different perspectives, different names. The television kept spewing them out. My parents called it "The End of Our Empire." Later on, Paolo and I would call it "The End of Our Family."

"You useless, worthless man! You stupid son of a bitch! You're driving us into poverty! Of all things, poverty! This is all your fault. What the fuck

are we going to do now? Puñeta! We've lost everything." *Bam!* Mama
slammed the door on Papa after her fit.

"Estrella, please stop screaming; you're scaring the kids. It's not my
fault. It's nobody's. Everyone who has money in the Middle East knows
that. Estrella, please, open the door," Papa begged Mama.

She opened the door and held a makeshift weapon—a fine-tooth
comb, a ruler, a lampshade—which he snatched from her hand and
threw on the floor. She slammed the door on him again, and we listened
to her scramble for something in the bedroom. When she had found
what she was looking for, she came out with it, holding it in front of
her face with arms in a V, her hair wet from sweat, her one sleeve off
the shoulder, and the object catching and reflecting light—her Spanish-
made, gold-finished letter-opener knife.

She took two steps toward Papa, paused, then tore through the
air between them with her stabbing. She stabbed the knife just an
inch away from Papa's ear, just barely missing his face. We all gasped
and froze—the maids who were covering our eyes and ears, the
personal assistant, the cook, the tutor, the gardener, Paolo, and me.
We watched Papa run for his life as Mama chased after him with
gold blade in hand. We watched her slash the air, just failing to
gash him by a centimeter or two. Papa, who grew up dodging wild
animal attacks in his penurious hometown, evaded Mama's acts of
violence by sprinting upstairs and hiding in the extra bedroom.
That night, he moved his belongings, too, and they were—physically
and emotionally—separated. Only our finances—or soon, the lack
thereof—bound them together.

I began wetting my bed.

After Papa moved upstairs, the mansion barely seemed like a palace
anymore. Flowers stopped adorning mantels one day, and the next, a car

was purchased off our lot. Dessert didn't come with lunch but just with dinner. The following month, there was no dessert at all. The maids started cleaning the house in unpressed clothes, and the drivers stopped waxing cars. Paolo's daily routine and my schedule dropped from three after-school activities down to just either piano or ballet. The gradual downsizing proved evident in every part of the house.

Papa made efforts to uplift the collective mood of the mansion. He wrote notes to me, Paolo, and Mama, and he taped them to our vanity mirrors. He took me to not just the ice-cream shop, but also to the ice-cream factory, and he took Paolo on Boy Scout campouts. He ate meals with the household staff, cracking jokes and retelling tales from his childhood: how he went to school with no shoes and how his family slept in between the ceiling and roof of the fish market. He told me, "This isn't normal. None of this is. But we were not made for normal. And for that, I am sorry."

He was home more often because he no longer had to travel for business. I liked seeing so much of him, how I could always ride piggyback on him and play tickle fight. Half of the time he was home, though, he was hiding from Mama or shaking his head and covering his ears from her screaming. Was he better off working, traveling many miles and flying first-class, away from us? I wasn't sure. I was still confused about babies and death and knives and all that screaming.

Papa noticed. He noticed how Mama had gone from dieting to starving, and how Paolo and I couldn't seem to get along. So he planned a swimming day at Palos Verdes, the members-only pool club on the Antipolo hill.

"Who wants to go swimming?" he said, as he and the drivers packed our Land Cruiser with coolers, towels, and snack baskets.

Paolo and I cheered.

"Okay! Hop in and pick out songs we can sing on our way up," Papa said.

"I have one! What about that one about puppies on the window?" I said.

"*In* the window, stupid. You can't be *on* a window," Paolo said.

I stuck my tongue out at him.

"Oh, you guys, come on. Let's keep it nice and fun," Papa said.

"Nice and fun, nice and fun," Mama said, mocking Papa as she sat in the middle-row seat, hiding behind her oversize sunglasses. She left her knife at home.

Papa rallied the maids and boys and had them pack coolers and led a convoy up the hill to Palos Verdes. We arrived at the club an hour later and were welcomed by perfect weather and bath-temperature water. It seemed like all we needed was some fresh air and time outside the mansion. Once there, Papa began grilling, showing Paolo and the boys how to properly start a fire. Everyone, including the help, stripped down to their bathing suits.

The women, on the other hand, gathered around to assist Mama—Judith lathering sunscreen on her back and legs, Dehlia untying her lace-up sandals, and Katring fixing her hair under a floral swim cap. Once prepped for the water, she shooed them away with a one-two flick of her fingers and strode toward me in her lipstick-red one-piece Valentino suit. I'd been giving my inflatable whale a bath on the side of the pool, scooping water with my bucket and pouring it over my blow-up friend. Mama told me to stop playing, to which I obliged.

"Come here," she said.

I put down my bucket and tiptoed to her.

Mama was a former collegiate swimmer. And her way of teaching us anything, including swimming, was to just throw us right in. Mama spun me around so that I faced the pool. She unbuckled my floatie, slid its Styrofoam rings off my arms, flung it about two meters away, and pushed me into the blue that was more than three meters deep. As I began to slip beneath the surface, she instructed everyone not to fish me out, to leave me room to struggle and gargle and kick my way up.

"You jump in to save her and you lose your job," she said, hands on waist.

She lectured them on how children learned by doing, and that the best and brightest, the leaders of our country and of the world, earned their ranks by nearly drowning. She didn't believe in lifesavers, not even in swim coaches, but in being hurled into whatever could kill you. As much as she and her ways were terrifying, they proved to be effective. Papa was getting ready to jump in, despite his lack of skill, but I kicked up and kicked up, my pan de sal thighs thrusting me up and my jamon de bola belly buoying me like a ship's hull. I learned to swim.

And I swam well.

After the knife incident, Mama lived as two people: Mama who hid a knife in her silk robe and yelled at Papa over every meal, and Mama who lured an audience among the maids with her graceful butterfly strokes and swan dives. She was Mama who broke carafes and saucers and urns, and Mama who hummed while wading.

When she waded and sunned, we acted like her other self was back at the mansion, far away from our singing and swimming, far away from the fire crackling in the grill, the bath-temperature water, the normalness of an afternoon at the pool. Paolo and I splashed and shot at each other with yellow-orange water guns and sang while we rode the inflatable whale. We cannonballed and raced to both ends of the pool, and when we ran short of breath, we hung on to the pool gutter to rest.

"Psst, come with me. I have a surprise for you," he said, pushing his body up on the gutter and out of the water.

"A surprise? What is it?" I said.

"Just come."

I tried to push up on the gutter like he did, but couldn't. I instead swam to the steps and climbed out. I followed him behind bushes, through the gate and to the playground, mulch and leaves sticking to my wet feet.

"Look, I found you the tallest, biggest slide in the whole world," Paolo said.

"Wow, that's really tall and really high, Kuya," I said.

"Go climb up and slide down."

"Let's go get Yaya."

"Tell you what, you go and then I go. Deal?"

I hesitated. Then I said, "Deal."

I walked around the slide and to the ladder, took a deep breath, and wiped my still-moist, wrinkly hands on my shorts. Then I wrapped my fingers around the stainless-steel rods and took one step up after the other, trying my best not to show how scared I was that the slide was three persons tall. I grabbed the bar on the edge of the platform, sat my rump on the cold metal ledge, and let go. The next second, I was in midair, legs over my head, arms flailing up to where I could reach a tree's branches. I suspended in the air for a couple of seconds, then banged my head on the cement floor.

The slide was missing a leg. Nobody, not even Paolo, knew. Instead of gravity pulling me down the slide and to the grass, it forced the top of the ramp—where I had just been sitting—to break off from the ladder and thrust skyward, flinging me like a projectile onto the pavement.

Mama ran screaming. She must've heard the slide fall and my skull smack the ground.

"Help!" Paolo said. He ran to my side and shook my arm, but I didn't respond. He tapped my cheeks and began crying. "Oh no, oh no, say something. Say something."

"Get the car! Get the damned car!" Papa said to the drivers.

I heard everyone cry and scream. I heard sandals flip and flop back and forth, the metal gate swing and shut, the car engine rumble. I heard ice swish around in a cooler and then felt it held to my head. I heard Lorna snivel and pray, "Diyos ko, let there be no blood."

"No blood, no blood," someone said.

"Stay with us, my darling girl," Papa said.

"She's not moving!" Mama cried.

She was right. I couldn't move. I thought about it and tried to raise my arm or wiggle a toe, to let them know I was okay, but I couldn't. I kept telling my hand to wave and my mouth to open, but nothing happened. I tried to swallow my spit, but saliva just foamed in the corners of my mouth and dribbled down my chin. I could see whatever was directly above me—faces, arms, my mother's hair falling in my face, the evening sky turning orange blue. I saw the evening's first stars, too.

I heard everything they were saying, but I couldn't respond. I heard the car backing up the driveway, the gates flinging open and closed, the maids praying to Jesus and Our Lady, Paolo sobbing and apologizing, Mama screaming at Papa and blaming him for the fall, Papa telling Mama, "Not now, please, not now!" and instructing the drivers to open the car door and start the engine.

I lay flat and stiff on Paolo's, Mama's, and Papa's laps in the back seat as we headed for the hospital. Mama couldn't get her bearings. She was just as paralyzed by the accident as I was. She sobbed. Her tears and wet hair fell on my face. They felt cold.

Typically, Mama could find a medical solution to anything, but this accident got the best of her. Paolo was still crying in the car, too. He kept saying, "Sorry, sorry. I didn't know, I didn't know."

Papa sang to keep me awake, calling me his sunshine and telling me I took away his gray skies. He looked straight into my eyes and I sang back to him in my head, in my heart. I wanted to tell him, *I'm scared.*

They took me to the nearest hospital, Santo Niño, where the lower class received medical care.

"She'll be fine," the doctor said. "Terrified and shocked, but she's fine." It was a skull injury, all on the surface—no concussions or brain damage at all, he said. Nothing too serious; I was just shocked. I had received a hard blow to the head when I hit the ground, but the ground didn't break my skull nor shake my brain. It was a closed head injury, only causing scalp wounds and a fist-size goose egg on the back of my head.

I was completely conscious but lay weak with vacant eyes, almost as if I had been put under a breath-holding spell. *Shock*, the doctor emphasized. *Shock*, the impact of the fall stunned me into silence and motionlessness. The doctor pulled my eyelids up and flashed a small light on my face.

"Are you sure?" Mama said, naming every possible diagnosis she'd read in pediatrics textbooks.

"I'm sure. She just needs to stay here until she's able to move and walk without assistance. We need to monitor her for twenty-four hours," the doctor said.

"Thank you, Doc," Papa said, giving him a pat on the shoulder.

I'd been wetting my bed, waking up sweaty from nightmares, and had become increasingly afraid of the dark. And now, *shock*, the doctor said.

My yaya had always said that children were very intuitive.

Something was wrong.

"This is all your fault," Mama said as soon as the doctor stepped out of the room.

"Estrella, *please*, our daughter almost *died*, for God's sake," Papa said in the angriest, most stern voice I'd ever heard him use.

Mama didn't care. She nagged and she yelled and they bickered.

Paolo walked up to the edge of the gurney.

"Why'd you have to scare us like that?" he said to me. "I thought you were gonna die there for a second."

I thought, *He loves me after all, that silly kid.*

"I promise to take care of you. I know I always trick you. I'm sorry. Here, you can have this."

Between my arm and torso, on the crisp white hospital sheets that smelled like Clorox, he tucked his most-prized possession: his Game Boy.

Common Enemy

Papa walked up the steps, calling out, "Where are my warriors?"

He passed my doorway, with a rolled-up world map in hand, and stepped into Paolo's bedroom. The map alone was invitation for me to join in, to drop the brush with which I had been combing my doll's hair, and to swoop out of my canopied bed, hurtle from my quarters to Paolo's, and lie on my stomach on my brother's Super Mario area rug.

Paolo sat with legs crisscrossed as Papa knelt between us and rolled out the map on the floor. He told Paolo to fetch his box of toy soldiers—the green army men my parents had brought back from Hong Kong.

"Do you know how armies are built?" Papa asked us as he pulled the soldiers out of the box and stood them on representations of land.

We shook our heads.

"Humans, by nature, will fight each other," he said. "Unless they are fighting the same cause or fighting the same bad guy, they're not likely to unite or peacefully coexist."

Paolo pointed at the plastic men standing over the word *China.* "These guys, Papa, who are they fighting together?"

"Perhaps the same dragon?" Papa said, making a claw with one hand and swinging it at the soldiers, forcing them off the continent and into the ocean.

"What about these guys, Papa?" I asked, picking up a soldier he had positioned on the shape that looked the most familiar to me—a kneeling man with hands in prayer, made up of many shapes and speckles—the Philippines.

"Our country is unique," he said. "It's made up of over seven thousand islands, of many different tribes, dialects, classes, and beliefs. There are big wars and small wars, visible and invisible ones."

"We're at war, Papa?" I said.

Paolo paused and set down the two soldiers he'd been banging against each other.

"Something like it," Papa said as he pulled us closer to him and sat us in his lap. With arms around us, he continued, "If you two band together, you can fight the Common Enemy. Now you two need to think about who and what you're against, because those things will either bring you together or tear you apart."

"You mean the war on TV?" Paolo said.

"That's one of them, one of the big ones."

"And people are dying? Killing each other with guns and grenades?" I said.

"Yes, but not everyone's killing each other with guns and grenades. Some of our men are dying of diseases at the camps."

"What camps?" Paolo and I said.

"Evacuation camps. They're not very clean, not a lot of space, not a lot of fresh air or safe food."

I didn't know how else to respond, so I got up, leaned forward, and pinched his cheeks and pulled at them, stretching his face to a clown's grin, and said in my G.I. Joe voice, "We are at war. And you, sir, are our captain!"

He and Paolo laughed, then transitioned onto all fours, hovering their bodies over the countries and continents, the soldiers and the seas.

They played combat the rest of the morning. I didn't know why, but I wanted to forget what Papa had just said: that we—our family, our country, and our world—were in some kind of war. I didn't like the goose bumps that appeared on my arms, nor did I like imagining any of us, especially myself, as one of the toy soldiers, armed and dangerous and in danger. I already had dead babies, broken slides, and Mama's knife to worry about. And now I was to worry about the Common Enemy, too. I ran back to my room, leaving Papa and Paolo, who were now wrestling each other and rolling on and off the map. I climbed into my bed, picked up the doll and her brush, and did what Mama did when she wasn't storming in or out of a room, or thundering at Papa about money in the Middle East: I brushed my hair a hundred strokes, no more and no less.

A week ago, Mama called Papa a failure, an ignorant peasant, and a "low-class fuckin' Indio." Afterward, she rolled a Chinese jade urn across the ballroom floor and through a French door, shattering the window and creating a crater where the urn landed. Mama had bouts of violence and anger and had pushed me into three meters of water, but I still somehow wanted to be near her.

I admired her for being a real-life doll: long legs, long arms, slim waist, shiny hair, and red lips. She was Rollerblade Barbie in the flesh—with lighters for skates, skidding against all that was beneath her and sparking a fire wherever she treaded. But still, when she wasn't ablaze, I drew to her like a bug to a flame. I believed that she was what I needed to keep warm: a glowing body.

After the hundredth brushstroke, I made my way to the master bedroom and found Mama reading in bed. She had *Vogue* on her lap and *Elle* in her hands, and sepia pictures and newspaper clippings spread out on the comforter. I sat on the davenport across from her and said nothing until she asked if I wanted to see some pictures. I snaked around the photographs, careful not to land my knee or the base of my hand on them. I fit my body between her pillow and what used to be Papa's. She set down her magazine, picked up a portrait of a man in a

European-style suit, a gentleman with Mama's and Tachio's eyes, nose, and lips, and said, "My father, your lolo, José Alarcon."

She reminisced about him—how he wore a suit and smoked cigars, had a car, and had a river named after him. He served as mayor of Rozal, her hometown, for over twenty-five years. She sat taller as she stated facts about him: his fluency in both Spanish and English, his blanco blood—a mix of Austronesian and Iberian—and his being part of the last generation of Ilustrados.

"Ilustrado. Say it with me."

"Ee-loos-TRAH-dō."

She stared at the picture and locked eyes with her father. "We are not like everyone else. Your grandparents were Ilustrados. Do you know what that means?"

"No, Mama," I said.

"It means our family ruled this country with the Spaniards. It means that you, because you are my daughter, have a special role in this country. It means that we are the educated ones, the ones who are fit to rule." She darted a glance at me. "This is who we are."

She went on about her father's politics: kindness to the masses and a large house for the missus justify corruption and crime. "It's how we do things up north."

"Was he kind to you?" I said.

She paused, then sniffed, and said, "However he was, I was his favorite."

Mama set Lolo's picture down and picked up a family portrait of five boys and four girls. She rubbed her thumb over a girl, about fifteen years of age, standing right in the center in a button-down bouffant dress. "That was me," she said. "Look how skinny I was. Having children ruined my body."

"But Mama, you're so beautiful. I don't think your body is broken, I mean ruined."

"You'll understand when you have children of your own." She rolled her eyes.

"Who are those other people?" I said, pointing at the two rows of teenagers in pressed outfits.

"My brothers and sisters. There were nine of us." She enumerated their names and explained the political or religious meaning behind each one: Benjamín, "son of my right hand"; José Junior, nicknamed "Jun"; Lupita, a diminutive of Guadalupe, referring to Our Lady of Guadalupe; Estrella, for the stars on the Philippine flag; Felipa, the most patriotic of the names; Demetria, after the Greek goddess of harvest and agriculture; Corazón, heart, courage, or patriotism; José Cristobal, after Christopher Columbus; José III also nicknamed Wayne, after John Wayne, and born in the 1950s, when American culture had swept through the country.

"I was the favorite," she said again. She recalled her father unabashedly declaring her as the prettiest of the girls, her sisters scowling and glowering at her high-bridged nose, straight hair, big hazel eyes, smooth mestiza skin, and her thin red lips. She told a story about Lolo parading her like a trophy and waving her like a flag at motorcades and campaigns. She shuffled through photos that confirmed her father's affections for her, that she, his precious Benny, was the gold sheen to his medal, the in-flesh manifestation of his patrician blood.

She started telling another story: one I had heard a couple of times before, about her first day of school. She'd been learning her numbers and letters at home.

"Oh, my Benny, it looks like you're ready to go to school," her father said.

"Yes, Papá, I want to go to school like my big brothers and big sister," young Estrella said.

"Okay, my Benny, I will take you to school and you will show me how smart you are."

Little mestiza Benny sat in her sister Lupita's class for an afternoon and wrote her name and sang songs and learned one-plus-one and two-plus-two. She raised her hand to ask questions and clarify points, sometimes contesting the teacher. She named all the rural towns and political districts of La Union and introduced herself to each first grader, shaking their hands and presenting herself as "Estrella, also called Benny, daughter of the longest-serving mayor of Rozal."

By the end of the day, she had earned the teacher's favor and a front-row seat in class. She had also earned the envy of her sister, who lagged behind her for years to come. From the first grade through her father's death in 1981, the year Paolo was born, Mama sat in the center of a world corrupted by politics, a world built on rice and tobacco farmers' backs, and a world made to bleed purple by several People's Revolutions.

By the time Mama had finished retelling tales from her childhood, tears had formed watermarks on some of the pictures. She pulled her knees into her chest and buried her face in them. First, she let out a sniff. Then let out a howl from her hollow womb. She sobbed, her shoulders quaking like they did the night of my third birthday, the night Tachio was born and immediately died. The bed shook with her, and the vibrations traveled up my back and neck. I was reminded of how she collapsed into the shaft of moonlight on the floor, wailing and trembling for her benumbed child.

"Mama, are you okay?" I said. "Tell me another story from when you were little."

"What?" she said. "Why are you here? Why aren't you in school?"

"Mama, I don't have school."

"Why not? Why are you here?"

"I'm here because you were telling me stories."

"Lorna! Lorna! Get her dressed! She's late for school!"

I scrambled out of her bed as she snapped out of Orchid Mama and into tiger mode.

Papa and Paolo played combat upstairs, while I fought to escape the conflict between Mama's personalities—Mama the fire versus Mama the flame.

This, too, was war.

Nightfall came. Fatigued from my day of learning about fighting, I requested just one bedtime story from Papa.

"One? It's like I don't even know you," Papa said.

"I'm tired, Papa. I did a lot today," I said.

"Well, what about a story about the fish market?"

What Papa lacked in pedigree, he made up for in character and tenacity. He was Indio inside and out, the poster child for everything that represented the Filipino plebeian: brown-skinned, flat-nosed, flat-footed from never having owned a decent pair of shoes. No one in his family had ever proved on paper whatever Spanish heritage he or his siblings claimed to have—they were either undocumented or fabricated. But no matter what colors or classes ran through my father's veins, he knew one thing to be true: he rebelled against the class system.

Papa had always been a great storyteller, a pro at turning any memory from his frugal childhood into an endearing fable. He rarely read picture books to us at bedtime because he had much better tales to tell. My favorite story was about him and his siblings living in the fish market, practically homeless, roughhousing and teasing and egging one another on like any other family.

"We had no money, but we were happy." Papa began all his stories this way. He sat on the bed between Paolo and me.

"What did you do as a kid? What made you happy?" Paolo and I asked him.

"Oh, the usual. We ran around—barefoot, of course—and we made fun of each other and called each other names. Your titos and titas called me 'goat' because I smelled and I didn't like to bathe," he said, clipping his nose with his index finger and thumb and pretending to gag.

"*Eeeeew*. Papa! Kids have to bathe!" Paolo said.

"Well, I told my sisters and brothers, 'You should thank me for not bathing: I'm leaving more water for you.'"

We laughed.

"Still, Papa, Mama says we should bathe twice a day."

"Your mama grew up rich. I had nothing."

For years, Papa and his parents and siblings didn't have a house. At night, after the fish market closed, they crawled up the market's scaffolding and squeezed between the ceiling and the roof, where they slept and kept the few things they owned.

"Was it dark? Were you scared?"

"It was dark and tight and hot and full of mosquitoes," he said. "We slept one skinny body next to the other, no space in between, like sardines in a can. Once you lay down, you couldn't get up, because there was no room to move."

"But were you scared?" I asked again, holding on to the edge of my blanket.

"Me? Scared? No way! My siblings and I made the most of what we had."

My father turned the dark into a place where he could imagine anything. In his mind, he said, they were royals! Papa placed his right hand on his chest and the left hand like a crown on the top of his head. "Royals from the Sultanate! Royals from Great Britain! Royals from the Arabian Desert!"

"Royals!" Paolo and I said.

"And you know what else made me feel like a king?"

"What, Papa, what?"

"One time, when everyone else was sleeping, I felt around for my sister's piggy bank. It was a rusty tin can sealed tight with masking tape and had a slot for coins. I needed money for candy, but I had spent all that I'd made from selling peanuts, so I thought I'd *borrow* her savings. And . . ."

"And what, Papa, tell us!"

"And while I fished for a centimo with a stick, I held my mouth open in anticipation of my prize, and . . ."

"What! What!"

"And the coin fell out of the can straight into my mouth and I choked on it! I choked on it for a good while, waking everyone up, until it passed through my throat and fell into the pit of my stomach. And there it stayed forever and ever!"

"Forever?" Paolo and I looked at each other.

"You bet. I can feel that cold coin in my stomach to this day, especially when I have my first cup of coffee in the morning. It's a great reminder of where I've been and where I wanted to be—of what I wanted to become. I never wanted to be poor again. I wanted to become a businessman and provide employment for people, provide for a family, build something big," he said, rubbing his stomach as if to search for the lost coin.

Paolo and I reached together for Papa's belly, feeling around for a dime-size bump. We fell asleep that way—our arms stretched across Papa's belly, our hands rising and falling with his breathing.

The smell of citrus polish woke me the next morning. The waxy orange scent perfumed the entire upstairs, the air hanging redolent over my comforter and face. I opened my eyes and mouth at the same time, unsticking eyelids and lips, feeling and tasting the product that had evaporated and thickened in our morning air. I sat up, sniffed, and discovered where it was coming from. Katring and Dehlia, the youngest of our servants, spun their hands left to right and right to left on the herringbone-patterned floor. They swirled their rags so fast, they created white blurs in the shape of eights. They exchanged chismes as they cleaned the floor, unaware that I had woken up and was listening.

"Nagsisikip ng sinturon," Katring warned Dehlia. Tightening of their belts.

"You know what that means—we're the youngest workers, the newest ones. Last to arrive, first to leave," Dehlia said.

They shook their heads.

"Maybe they'll keep us because we're younger, faster. Lorna can barely lift the little ones on and off their beds. She can hardly walk up the mansion's steps without panting," Katring said.

"We just have to keep working harder. No breaks. Maybe sir will notice."

Katring wiped her sweaty forehead on her sleeve, let go of her rag for a second, and clasped her hands in prayer. "I don't want to go back to the province. You know what could happen to me."

I didn't understand what she meant, but could tell by how tight she held her hands together and how she waxed the floor to an unbelievable sheen that whatever fate awaited her in her province was much less desirable than her already-lowly station at the mansion.

I yawned and cleared my throat to get their attention.

"Good morning, Neng," Dehlia said. "Just polishing the floor."

"I know, I can smell it." I inhaled. "Smells like oranges. Makes me hungry. Will you call my yaya for me so I can get changed? You might have to help her up the steps—she's so old and slow, don't you think?"

Katring's jaw dropped and Dehlia covered her mouth with her wax-covered hand.

I smiled at them, pulled an imaginary zipper across my mouth, and said, "I won't tell, I promise. She *is* getting really pudgy and sluggish. Sometimes I have to help her when she's helping *me* get ready." I rounded my arms and rolled from side to side on the bed and puffed up my cheeks like a balloon, making Katring and Dehlia laugh.

We prayed before breakfast. Papa blessed our meal and thanked God for the bounty. He said, "Make us content with what we have and prepare us for whatever may lie ahead."

Mama interrupted. "Lord, keep us where we belong. We do not know how to be anywhere else. Please bless us—in the best high-class possible way—for as long as the Republic lives."

Paolo took a turn and asked for more Nintendo games, an air gun, and a bucket of Green Slime. He would've kept petitioning for more toys for himself, so I interjected.

I said, "God, I need a new hairbrush. And . . . I just want everyone to stop fighting. Amen."

The room quieted. No one spoke while we ate. We made no sounds except for the *clank* of forks and spoons against plates. I ate much but quickly, then excused myself and headed downstairs.

Where the servants lived, a different type of crusade took over. There transpired a Holy War composed of different sides and many opposing petitions. Lorna, Angge, and Judith prayed the rosary on their knees in the servants' hall, moving their thumbs along a string of beads as they repeated the Hail Mary and the Lord's Prayer, asking, petitioning, begging that they would be able to keep their jobs. Katring and Dehlia stood at the doorway, uninvited to the three older women's prayer circle.

I pulled on Katring's shirt and made a funny face. She giggled and tickled my side and asked if I wanted to practice my letters with her. She propped me up on the kitchen table and pulled out a legal pad Papa had given her. I wrote my name, and she wrote hers, and I called out words like *aso*, *pusa*, *kuting*. Dog, cat, kitty. She sounded out the syllables and jotted them down letter by letter. And I commended her for each one she got right.

"Ang galing natin magsulat, Ate Katring." We're good at writing, big sister Katring.

She gave me a hug and said, "And you—you are another reason why I don't want to leave this mansion."

I rested my head on her shoulder and said, "I don't want you, or anybody, to ever leave. I don't know why you keep saying that."

"Oh, forget I said anything," she said, squeezing me hard and sighing.

"Dehlia! Katring!" We heard Mama beckon. It was time to clear the breakfast table.

Back on the main floor, Mama and Papa sat across from each other. Dehlia picked up plates and loaded them onto a tray. Katring wiped the table with a vinegary rag as I sat in my chair and listened to my parents' conversation. Papa explained to Mama that our supplies had started to run low. We were down from tens of millions to just a couple of them. According to his computations, Mama had to cut her couturier, Mr. Albrando, off the budget and resort to buying ready-to-wear.

"It's your choice—another cocktail dress, or a maid waiting on you and keeping your house clean. Imagine what your aerobics friends would say if they came over and the house was a mess and there was one less servant to send on an errand," he said.

"Makes sense," Mama replied, thumbing through her Rolodex for Mr. Albrando's phone number. "I'll close my couturier account, but I *have* to keep all the shoes I own now."

"All right," Papa said, leaning back into his chair.

Katring smiled at Dehlia and me. They took the trays downstairs with shoulders back and heads held high, now unencumbered by the possibility of unemployment.

"Hup, two, three, four. Hup, two, three, four," I said.

"What's the matter with you?" Paolo said. "*Stop* marching behind me."

"You're the leader and I'm the G.I., like G.I. Joe, so I have to follow you and your orders," I said.

"Well, I order you to get away from me," he said. "Wait a second. What do you know about G.I. Joe? Have you been playing with *my* toys?"

"At the hospital you said I could play with your toys. Remember, I almost died and you gave me your Game Boy and you said I could . . ."

"Blah, blah, blah," he said, cutting me off. "But you can't break them, okay?"

"Okay," I said, then paused for a minute and adjusted the gun belt I had fashioned out of construction paper. I mumbled, "Hey, if you want, I can make you a gun belt, too."

Paolo looked away, avoiding my glance like he usually did, then peered at my belt from the corner of his eye.

"It does look awesome. You've always been creative like Papa," he said. "But yeah, it's cool."

"Okay, cool. I'll make you one," I said. "A really cool one."

"Okay, I guess we can be cool together," he said, now looking at me. "Like a kid army."

I spent the afternoon cutting and gluing strips of construction paper and measuring them around my waist. I posed in front of the mirror in the upstairs hallway, pretending to pull a gun from my belt and firing at my reflection, blowing smoke off the weapon's barrel and once again firing at the soldier in front of me.

Paolo stepped out of his room, eager to see what I had made for him. He told me he loved it and ordered me to bring him all the pillows I could find. I lugged bolsters, neck rolls, throw pillows, body pillows, and down pillows from every room. We built a fort at the end of the hallway, between my room and his.

"*Bang! Bang!* I shot him!" Paolo said as he peered out of our pillow fort, aiming his gun—his middle finger and thumb—at our pretend enemy.

"There's more of them! Here, throw the grenade," I said, handing him a bottle of baby powder.

He hurled the bottle overhead and counted, "One . . . two . . . three . . ."

"*BOOM!*" we said together.

Then we high-fived, stood up, turned around, and saw what a mess our grenade had made. Talcum dust covered every inch of the upstairs hallway. Our jaws dropped in shock at first, but it didn't take long for us to find humor in the havoc—the havoc we made *together*. We snickered and snickered until our snickers turned into snorts.

"Kuya," I said, interrupting our fun, "so who do you think is our Common Enemy?"

He looked out again at the filth before us, made a fist with one hand and punched it into the other, and said, "Whatever it is that makes us unhappy."

Elma

Elma was our laundrywoman's daughter, the youngest of nine. She looked, as my yaya put it, short-of-seven-soap-baths-darker than I was, almost black. She had a "cookie face"—round, flat, with barely a nose, and no forehead. She didn't have thighs, just long, narrow pipes with scabbed, blotchy knobs for knees.

Her parents came from a Philippine province called Bicol, where sweet pili nut and giant Saba bananas grew, an impoverished region painted with natural beauty from sea line to mountaintop. My parents, as most people from our class, only visited the place for logging and farm-fishing opportunities.

In Bicol, the people ate very spicy food—as if their taste buds were direct descendants of the local Mayon, an active, but perfectly conic volcano. Although lovers of picante food, Bicolanos have a reputation for studied calmness and for rarely showing their rough edges. As we Tagalogs would say, Sa loob ang kulo. The boil is inside. They are a people who care, bend, and sway. They don't like trouble.

Elma's parents left all but two of the oldest boys in Bicol when they first started working for us. Her parents, Manang Biday and Manong Bidoy—as my parents had named them—washed our clothes, cared

for our plants, cleaned our cars, and when necessary, killed snakes that
lived in our trees or swam in our toilets. Her two brothers, our "boys,"
swept, mopped, and raked outside. Cleaning inside was a task reserved
for help of higher ranks.

Manang Biday's kids had been writing about what a terrible time
they were having with the neighborhood drunks. The old lady wanted
to spare her youngest the humiliation and sexual harassment. So she
took Elma on a six-hour bus ride to Manila that bright Saturday morning, and convinced my parents that her daughter could be an extra set
of hands and feet to send on errands—for free.

Elma was eight when I first met her, and I was six, but because she
was born many classes under me, she spoke to me with formality and
respect.

"Good morning, po," she said, a word added to the end of a sentence to make it formal, respectful, obliging.

"What's your name?" I said, forgetting that her first language wasn't
English, because she was from the lowest class.

"Po?" she said.

"Your name. Ano'ng pangalan mo?"

"Elma."

I smiled at her and took her hand. Surprised, she let go. She'd never
held the hand of anybody from my family or class before.

"It's okay," I said. "Halika, let's play. You like taguan?"

"Opo," she said. Yes. What kid doesn't like hide-and-seek?

I whisked her away to the upstairs part of the house, where we
played hide-and-seek all day. Once we'd used all hiding spots upstairs,
we changed the rules of the game and expanded our playing field to the
entirety of the mansion.

"We can hide anywhere but inside the urns. There are witches and
dead babies there," I said, in the kind of Tagalog my yaya spoke: deep,
hard, and without a trace of Western education.

"Wan, too, trrree, pohrr, payb, seeks, sebem . . . ," she counted in English, her consonants forcing through her sharp, crooked, mouselike teeth as they would in her staccato-sounding dialect.

"Woo-hoo, I'm here! Come find me," I said, calling out to the It from behind the curtain or under the table.

"Ha! Boom!" she said. "Ha! Boom! Found you!"

I shared my snacks with her, as Papa said I should. But I was careful not to let her on my bed. "They're dirty," Mama had said. "They don't even have shoes. Don't let them on your bed, you understand?"

I showed her the two dolls I was allowed to play with, the only two that weren't encased behind glass.

"This is Calbolite, *kalbo* for bald," I said, handing her a hairless Cabbage Patch Kid doll.

"Nakakatawa naman," Elma said. How funny.

"This is Tiffany," I said. "She's American, so her name is Tiffany."

"Tee-pah-nee? I've never heard of that name. And American? Why American?"

"My daddy brought her from the States. States, do you know what that is?"

"Ah, oo. Eees-teyts. Eeestate-side. Imported." The words *States* and *imported* were familiar and interchangeable to us post-Marcos kids. We came from a nation and generation heralded as the most pro-American in the world.

"I'll play mom and you'll play nanny," I said, coaching her through every second of our playdate.

We played all morning and afternoon. I made her laugh a few times. Every time she laughed at my jokes, I wanted to tell my brother, who was at soccer practice, *I told you: I'm a funny girl!*

Elma's every giggle boosted my self-esteem. Her being darker than I was made me feel good about myself—I wasn't *so* dark after all. I wanted to be like her, if not *be* her. I watched how tightly she hugged her mom every time Manang Biday came to check on us. I watched her be riddled with amazement at her first encounter with a kaleidoscope. I watched her scarf down biscuits and pan de sal rolls I'd been warned not to eat too much of. I watched her put together a puzzle I'd been bored with, or play with a broken toy I'd kicked around. I watched her press my drapes and skirts against her cheeks, as if she'd only ever touched soiled rags. I watched her run. I'd never been a runner, and I envied that of her. She could sprint away from whatever troubled her.

"Elma! Elma!" her mother called out to her.

I turned my head.

"Dali! Quick!" I said, as I grabbed her hand and led her down the steps, through the long dark hallway and into the basement. I shoved her into the closet under the stairs and shut it locked.

"Hoy! Hoy!" she started yelling at me in an informal way. "Why am I in here?"

In my panic, I started yelling back at her in straight English, which she couldn't understand.

"Just hide! Stay in there! Stay! Be my friend, *stay!*"

She coughed and struggled for air in the closet.

"Shh! Shh! It's *real* hide-and-seek now. You're hiding; they're seeking. Get it? So, shh!"

"Elma! Elma!" her mother called out again.

"What's happening here? Biday, ano 'to?" my mother said as she walked out of the master bedroom in her lazy Saturday robe.

"I can't find Elma, mam," Manang Biday said.

"Boy! Boy!" my mother called out to our male servants, Manang Biday's sons. "Look for your sister! Dali!"

I heard the scurry of their steps as they searched the house for Elma. They looked upstairs and downstairs with flashlights in hand, never noticing that I was also hiding. They didn't think to look in the basement, my mother's clothes closet, because they didn't think Elma would know where the secret door was. That's why I hid her there. *Told you I'm more than just book-smart. I'm street-smart, too,* I wanted to tell my brother. He was always making fun of how sheltered I was and how little I knew of the real world. He was wrong. I knew about people from the outside. And I knew how to get them to do things for me, like hide and stay.

But that was gone when my mother came to the basement for a change of clothes.

"Shhh! Shhh! Shhh!" I said with my mouth against the closet door, shushing Elma, who was still coughing inside the cubby.

"What are you doing here?" my mother said.

"Nothing."

"What is *that*? Who is that coughing? Is that the laundrywoman's daughter?"

"No, no. I don't know. Mama, no!" I said, as she pushed me out of the way and opened the closet door. Elma emerged wheezing, blue black from not being able to breathe. I turned just as blue when I saw her face. I thought I'd killed her.

"Bidaaay! Biday!" my mother said, yelling up at the ceiling, toward the main floor.

"Mam, mam, mam, yes, mam," Manang Biday said as she nearly fell down the steps, rushing to her daughter's rescue and my mother's fury.

"Why is *this* here? This one's going to steal jewelry, isn't she?" my mother said, holding Elma by her sleeve.

"Naku, mam, she's not," she said to my mother. "Elma, anak, okay ka lang?" She stroked Elma's forehead over and over, like a newborn being hushed to sleep. Elma's arms were tied around her mother's waist, still heaving but slowly recovering from her near suffocation.

"I'm sorry, Elma," I said crying, reaching my hand out to her. "I just wanted you to . . ."

"Go!" my mother said, interrupting my plea. "Next time something like this happens, that one can't stay here."

"Sorry, po, mam. It won't happen again. Please forgive us, please. Elma, apologize."

"Sorry, po, mam Doctora," Elma said with a scratch in her throat. "Pasensiya na po."

"Hunh. Sa susunod, you'll lose your job, you'll see," my mother said, as she inspected her boxes of jewels. "Ingrata. I let your family live in the back lot for free and you repay me with this ridiculousness? Hmm."

Speechless, Elma and I both cried. She cried to her mom, into the sweaty side of her batik cleaning dress, while I cried running away from the scene. I ran—at least I tried to—upstairs and to my bed. And I was alone again, with no one to play with.

Gilded

Money dwindling, my parents should've walked away from the mansion, but instead they decided to prettify it with the last bit of wealth we had. "A beautification project," Mama called it. "An investment," Papa said. And so it was born: Mansion Royale, a grand palace.

That summer, Mama rehired her decorator, whom she had laid off the same week she sold the his-and-hers Rolexes, Omegas, and Pierre Cardins; the same week our accountant and lawyers gave their two weeks' notice, stating that they foresaw our family no longer affording their services. The decorator came, salivating as he walked up the grand staircase, carrying and fumbling fabric swatches, furniture brochures, and gold tassels—tassels that swished side to side, glistening in the tropic sun and in the light from our chandeliers. The tassels swished and swayed like the purple-clad decorator's hips and swung in alternating tempos like his hand. *Magical*, I thought, my eyes widening at the sight of tufts of braided gold thread.

"Don't touch," Mama said. "You can look, but you can't touch. These are very important samples."

"Oh, yes, Madam Doctora is right. Very important, very expensive," the decorator said. "Not for little girls, but for ladies . . . like us."

He and Mama tittered as they plunged back into the chaise lounge sitting before the table of ornaments, their feet splayed out and thrown up into the air.

I took a tassel and stuffed it into my ruffled-lace socks. Mama and her clotheshorse friend didn't notice, their eyes busy perusing brochures and their mouths forming oohs and aahs. I skipped upstairs, my new toy tickling my ankle.

I modeled in front of the hallway mirror outside Paolo's bedroom, styling the tassel on my hair, in my hair, and hanging down my fore-head as if an extension of my hairline part. I wore it on my belt, on the tongue of my shoe, and in the pinch between my shoulder and sleeve.

"For ladies, like us," I said, blowing kisses at the mirror.

"You're crazy," Paolo said.

"No. I'm Mama," I said, with one hand on my hip and the other holding the tassel in front of my mouth as if to feed myself grapes.

The next morning, I woke up hungry for breakfast, only to find no food on the breakfast table. Instead, Papa's ledgers and blueprints and yellow pads covered what would've been a spread of pan de sal, fried egg, dried fish, and garlic-fried rice. Papa and Mama stood over the table, fingers scratching chins and pointing at "Plan A," "Plan B," and "Pros and Cons" drafted on the papers. I hadn't seen them standing next to each other in months, much less agreeing with each other and not screaming.

"Where's the food?" I said.

"Good morning, darling girl," Papa said. "How's my good luck charm doing this morning?"

"Hungry."

"Hungry? Oh, well, we have no time to be hungry this morning. Today we start our next big project."

"Our what?"

"Our next big project: Mansion Royale! A Grand Palace!" Papa said, looking around the half-decorated breakfast room and half-ornamented disco hall and waving his arm in one big swoosh, as if presenting a newly knighted squire.

My yaya handed me a roll of pan de sal, sat me in a rattan chair, and brushed my hair. As she brushed the hundred strokes my mother had primarily hired her to do, my yaya explained that Mama and Papa were transforming the mansion into a function hall, a place where the upper-middle class, or as Mama put it—*the newly rich*—could host weddings, debuts, birthday parties, and banquets. For a fee and a booked date, Yaya said, the public could experience the grand life we supposedly lived. They could dance under our disco ball, waltz under the chandeliers and puzzle of mirrors, and dine while being served by our household staff.

"But this is *our* house!" I said, crossing my arms while munching on the roll.

"They need many money," Yaya said in English. "Many money to save house. People want to live like you and your brother, want to see inside house."

"Why would they want to live like us? Mama and Papa are always fighting, I have no friends, Paolo screams at Mama the way Mama screams at Papa. I don't get it."

"Then don't get. Just eat. Eat."

That about ended the conversation, and before long, Mama instructed us to leave the main floor and to wait upstairs until "everything's ready."

For days, Paolo and I ate our meals in bed and played in our upstairs fort, not allowed to set foot on the main floor and garden. Finally, after nearly a week of eavesdropping on the clinking, clanking, and moving,

Paolo and I stepped out of our rooms, fetched by Papa to see the obra maestra they had created below.

"Ta-da!" Papa said, his presenting arm once again spread out like a king's. "What do you think?"

Paolo and I stood bemused at the foot of the steps, our heads tilting from side to side, as if to inspect something that had been turned upside down.

The jade urns glowed, the marble floors in the ballroom and the terra-cotta tiles in the breakfast room smelled of citrus-scented polish, and the chandeliers sparkled alternately with the tassels—hundreds of tassels—hanging from every bit of architecture and trim. High-top tables lined the perimeter of the ballroom, and where the oval dining table used to be, a rectangular fourteen-seater now welcomed guests with bone china and stemware. Flowers once again adorned consoles and tea tables, perfuming the mansion with the smells of years past: Hawaiian gardenia, jasmine, daphne, bird-of-paradise, and, of course, orchid.

"It's so . . . so . . . shiny," we said together.

"We're already so popular. Our first guests arrive tonight—an engagement party," Mama said as she leafed through her black leather-bound Filofax. "Then two days from now, a wedding, and then an eighteenth-birthday debut. The next weekend, we have another wedding, then a launch for some nutritional product, then the week after we have my aerobics friend's fortieth birthday, then another debut *with* a full cotillion . . ." Mama carried on, flicking the pages of her organizer. She called out words to the air again.

"Cotillion!"

"Etiquette!"

"Debutante!"

"Corsage!"

That night marked the beginning of my nightly lockup with Paolo. He and I remained cooped up upstairs while hundreds of strangers elbowed one another through the main doors.

We spied on the festivities below from the top of the stairs, sometimes scrunching our faces through the handrails to see the ball gowns, tuxes, and traditional barongs making merry on the main floor.

My favorite of the events were the debuts, the eighteenth-birthday balls given to daughters who, Mama said, "were no longer girls, but ladies." The birthday girl received roses from eighteen suitors and wish candles from eighteen female friends. She walked up and down the red-carpeted main staircase in a ballooning gown frilled with bows and lace, escorted by the suitor she found to be most attractive and suitable for her class and kind. "Prinsesa," Elma and I called her, charmed by her sashay across the ballroom floor.

Equally admiring and envious, Elma and I sat in the guest room balcony with our sketch pads, drawing the sparkling scenes that interrupted our home life. I drew each princess, paying attention to every detail—from the width of a pleat and the curlicue of a ruffle, to the height of her coiffed hair and the point of her kitten-heel shoe. But I drew the tassels hanging around the house and surrounding the princess with the most effort, drafting and then erasing, drafting and then erasing, until I got every golden strand right.

"No, Elma. This strand flicks to the right, that braid swings to the left. The ones hanging in the disco room swish with the air blowing from the big fan. See?" I held up my stolen tassel to show Elma how the golden adornments swung.

Some nights, the parties lasted until daybreak, which meant that if Paolo and I pretended to sleep long and believably enough, we could dress ourselves in our Sunday fashions and sneak downstairs and mingle. Paolo zipped through the crowd to the turntables, asking the DJ if he could teach him to spin. I shimmied through the promenade of goblet-toasting guests, finding my way to the ballroom where I used to play princess. At seven years, I was half the height of most guests and couldn't see around the room filled with parading and waltzing bodies. But then I remembered to look up at the puzzle of mirrors ceiled above.

And there it was, my beloved kaleidoscope, a jamboree of boutonnieres, shoulder pads, pastel to neon dresses, and suits as black as the coifs dancing near them: a human carousel. They spun and spun, and I circled with them. For a stolen second, I twirled in my petticoat skirt like the princess I was rumored to be. And at mid-twirl, voilà! It was over.

"What are you doing here?" Yaya said as she hoisted me out of the ballroom. "Naku! Your mama will be mad. Come on, before we get caught!"

Mama had an industrial kitchen built in the back lot, pushing the boundaries of Elma's family's shack into a tighter squeeze of space. Manang Biday and her children's living space, as they understood, now extended into the restaurant-size kitchen, which meant that now they were not only to wash our clothes, mop our floors, and trim our grass. They were to chop vegetables, butcher meat, rind lemons, and peel Saba bananas as well. Mama, of course, did not leave all cooking operations for Mansion Royale to Manang Biday's ingenuity and ability to adapt. She hired a chef: Sid, a dark-skinned plump man with a mole on the cleft of his chin, who used to cook on luxury liners.

The maids loved Sid. He talked about his travels to Qatar, to Indonesia, and once, to Alaska. He knew how to make delicacies from elsewhere: couscous and tabbouleh from the Mediterranean, croque-madame from France. He sang while stirring, jived while he julienned. He said, "It's not important! I'm here now—to serve you lovely ladies," every time the maids asked why he stopped working on ships. The maids quickly forgot the question, smitten by his cultured ways.

Apart from cooking, Sid also trained the waitstaff. He showed them how to make swans and rosettes out of napkins, and how to pin-tuck a tablecloth into a drape of pleats and diamonds. Unfortunately, Papa said, training the staff wasn't Sid's strong suit. The napkins he and the maids folded often slumped like sloths, or coiled, not like roses, but snails. The pintucks looked more like a wrinkled curtain than a cascade of precisely angled geometric shapes. Papa had to hire someone who had the skills of a maître d'hôtel—Lancho.

Lancho stood straight all the time. His body was erect as one flat ironing board from head to foot, not one joint bent from knuckles to toes. His black serving tux stretched from one bony shoulder to the other, making Sid's white chef suit look like a sad case of a rice sack. Lancho set tables with the help of a meter stick, and not only folded napkins but also ironed them. He walked around with a clipboard, always smiling but never showing his teeth. I never heard his voice because he only ever spoke to Mama and Papa, and only by whispering to them over their shoulders. Mama and Papa always responded with a nod, or "Well, of course."

Sid, on the other hand, half-snorted most of his sentences while chewing on a toothpick. Paolo and I found the two hired men funny. One reminded us of a Siamese cat, and the other, a pug. They kept us entertained like the pets Paolo and I had always wanted.

"It's still not enough," Papa said, as he *tsk-tsk*ed over the ledger.

"What do you mean, not enough?" Mama said, ripping the ledger out of Papa's hands. "This is impossible."

The upkeep of the mansion and the overhead for the function hall, Papa explained, depleted much of the cash flow. "The cost of lighting up and air-conditioning the house alone is killing us," he said. "We have to expand."

For another week, Mama and her decorator instructed the help to repaint, repolish, and move furniture. The male servants emptied the master bedroom of personal items, transferring jewels, cosmetic kits, neckties, and robes to the basement. Without choice, but also without much hesitation, Mama and Papa made the matrimonial suite accessible to the public. The public, however, found it peculiar to be spending the night in my parents' bed. Mansion Royale: A Grand Palace garnered little bed-and-breakfast type of attention, and the only other way to make an income off the master bedroom was to turn it into a film set.

"Lights! Camera! *Akkkk-syon!*" I heard some man yell into a large cardboard cone. As soon as the baseball-capped man yelled his three words, the mansion—strangers, staff, and residents alike—quieted and froze. Then a mustached man would break the silence with a "Honey, I'm sorry" or an "Anak ng puta!" Then we would hear moaning, or sometimes moaning, then screaming, then moaning, and after a minute or so of sheets rustling, "Cut!" the man with the cone would yell.

"What are they doing, Yaya?" I said, scrunching my face through the handrails on the steps.

"Make teleserye. My show. My peyborit show," she said of the production, which was called *Ana Luna, Mara Clara, Clara Ana, Ana Clara,* or some other combination of those names.

"So the man and the woman are just pretending to sleep and play in Mama and Papa's bed?"

"Ay naku! Shh! No more questions. Makulit."

Cameras, costumes, big lights, small lights, fake guns, microphones, reflectors, extension cords, tripods, and scripts trailed our floors and took over what used to be a space for playing. Our kitchen help made chafing dish after chafing dish of food for the cast and crew, fashioning a catering service out of the back-lot kitchen. The maids still in our employ relished lunch and coffee breaks, as they had the opportunity of serving and coming close to a movie or teleserye celebrity. Some members of the household staff were lucky enough to be chosen as extras:

the drivers playing themselves in big-screen productions, driving the
don or doña up or down the driveway.

Daytime brought in strangers with cameras, large microphones,
and cardboard cones, while sundown marked the opening of wrought-
iron gates to strangers paying to party. I heard one of the crew say to
Mama and Papa, "What a majestic place, talaga. Must be magical living
here, diba?"

Mornings and afternoons mimicked elaborate breakfasts with
Mama, although without the softness and stillness I associated with
those early moments of the day. Dusk until dawn resembled my third
birthday party—the sparkling of champagne glass towers, the plush-
ness of couture gowns and red carpets—but without the quiet ending
of Tachio's death.

Some nights Paolo sat with me and Elma on the balcony, all three
of us ducked behind the rail, to watch the dancing and parading and
champagne-glass toasting taking place in the garden. Our stalking from
our would-be tower made us privy to what was unseen below: a truck
piled high with chafing dishes, glassware, and décor, parked to the left
of the wrought-iron gates, and Lancho and Sid hauling rice sacks of
goods and siphoning the last of my parents' capital.

I twiddled with my tassel while viewing the spectacular show that
was Mansion Royale. The more I fidgeted with the golden tuft, the
more it came undone. Braids untwisted, threads thinned out. Soon
the tassel was merely a fray—a fringe no longer gilded, an unhemmed
bunch of loose thread.

With Our Lady looking over the festivities and our dead baby
brother lying underfoot, strangers lived what they thought were our
lives—ball gowns, boutonnieres, scenes, and sights; a mansion bedaz-
zled, bewildering, but a dream.

Forty Days

Papa sat with me and Elma at the top of the main staircase, the three of us looking out at the haze of gray rolling in as frogs hopped on and off the steps while bloating their throats. The Bermuda grass in the garden undulated and swayed to the amphibians' croaking, while the maya birds took shelter in the gables.

Elma and I had been playing jacks that morning, bouncing the rubber ball and swiping plastic asterisks off the marble floor. Papa joined us, sipping his morning coffee, singing "You Are My Sunshine," and at times interrupting our play by cupping his hand over the ball, catching it, bringing it to his mouth, and pretending to swallow it whole. Elma and I laughed each time, and then begged for him to give us back our toy.

"If you tell me a joke, you can have your ball back," he said.

"Oh, me! Me! I have one!" Elma and I both said, raising our hands. We told jokes until thunder made an interruption.

And then it came: that sensation of a lick on the back of the ear, dampness on the brow, and eyes glossed and eyelids heavy with dew. Papa's metallic-framed glasses fogged up, the polished jade urns sweated, clamminess swarmed in my shirt and all around.

The storm announced itself again with thunder. And with it, flickers of light touched the ground. A wind rushed toward us from beyond the mansion's stone walls and over the green garden, and cycloned up the steps and to the landing. My plastic asterisks and rubber ball whisked off the marble floor, and away they went toward the storm, *bloop-bloop-bloop* down each step.

The noxious Philippine heat gave way. The earth laid its plains flat and ready for the pouring of rain, the watering of crops, and the quenching of thirst. The pond and rice paddy next door swelled up, and the farmer and his sons cried out—so loud that we in the mansion could hear them from the other side of the stone wall—"Salamat sa Diyos!" Thanks be to God. They rain-danced in their rolled-up jeans and cotton camisetas, welcoming Mother Nature's gift from above. The nuns hauled potted plants and chairs on rickshaws into the convent and pulled shut their holy doors. The plants and trees once again had something to drink. The mammals of the land and the birds of the air could cool down. The frogs puffed up their throats as if to exclaim, *Hallelujah!*

Papa, on the other hand, shook his head. "We've needed this rain, but this'll be more than what we need. Elma, find your mother and brother. Tell them to pack up."

Elma found her mother and brother, and along with a few of the maids they rescued Mama's clothes, shoes, and accessories from the basement closet—whatever hadn't been sold to a friend or auctioned off at an off-site estate sale. They bagged jewelry boxes, Hermès bags, and dozens of pairs of Christian Dior and Salvatore Ferragamo stilettos, espadrilles, ankle boots, and kitten heels. Yaya and Manang Biday unhooked dozens of hangers holding blazers, dresses, and puff-sleeved blouses. They threw them into wicker hampers and suitcases, and lugged them to the main floor with the might that belonged only to the low-class laborer.

Papa kept grinding his teeth and clenching his jaw. He said under his breath, "Good god, no. This is a Pacific rain—the kind that drowns all things."

I hugged his leg and rested my weight on his side. Together we watched as land and sky stared at each other, as land and sky became hard to tell apart. Each reflected the water hole that it faced. The drips kept coming, faster and harder each time, as the water found all the mansion's cracks and creases, and spilled and sloshed its way throughout and through-in. The water came from all sides, first dashing through the back-lot kitchen, taking down with it stacks of plates, chafing dishes, table linens, goblets, champagne flutes, silver trays, pots, and pans. Then it circled in closer and closer, until the entire downstairs—the garden, the driveway, the maids' quarters, the parking lot and back lot, the gym, and Mama's basement closet—was submerged. Waves of brownish-white froth thrashed from bank to bank, from one side of our thirty-million-peso fort to the other. A ring of foam wrapped itself around our tropical manor, warning: *Two and a half meters of water. Sink or swim.*

Papa paced back and forth while saying, "This is not happening. We're already drowning."

While most of Mama's prized belongings made it to dry land, some disappeared into the water—the great cleanser. The grown-ups clicked their tongues as they salvaged what they could, hauling pieces—broken or whole—to higher ground, where they thought they'd be safe.

Elma's father, Manong Bidoy, reported to my father and said, "Some poor people have drowned; some rich people have fled. What should we do, sir?"

Mama and Papa decided to stay put. The flood had already made an island out of us. My family and the help stayed on the main and upstairs floors, sharing space and air in a way we never had before. My family slept in our respective bedrooms, while the household staff was instructed to camp on the ballroom floor. I wanted Elma to sleep in my bed with me, but my yaya reminded me that Elma was dirty and ran around with no shoes—she certainly was not allowed on my linens.

The storm did not stop. It forced us to amuse ourselves indoors for days, weeks, or what Papa called, "these goddamn forty days." Sometimes the power went out and stayed out for fifteen, twenty, forty, ninety minutes. Sometimes it stayed out for a whole night. The monsoon gave me my first experience of candlelit living, of darkness being larger than our upper-class life.

When morning came, Elma and I played. We found sticks and string to make fishing poles with. We tied the parts together—tight, so the current couldn't break them. Then we lowered our tools, our simple machines, dangling them down from the terrace to the sea beneath. A slipper, a bicycle tire, a can, a necklace, and a satin ribbon from Mama's basement closet were our catch of the day. While fishing, Elma and I snagged what Mama called "bottom-feeders": catfish, flatfish, eel. Elma choked our catch with her thick-skinned hands, ripped it off the hook with no remorse, and held it up to my face and said, "Smell it. That is what fish smells like."

I gagged, but I giggled. I giggled because I'd done something Mama would never do or approve of, but something Papa was accustomed to. Something he had done as a child. *That is what fish smells like.* It was the same smell that swarmed through the wet market he grew up in, the pungent, striking stink that said, "Welcome home."

Elma's family's shanty, a square made of cardboard and corrugated tin, soaked in the back lot. It steeped in the earth's sweat and tears, coloring it brown like a tea bag in hot water. Its bits withered until most of the primitiveness was gone.

"Elma! Your things!" I said, pointing at the deterioration.

"Okay lang," she said, "I saved the important things. Anything else we own is trash."

She mounted a chair on a table, climbed up on it, and reached for the gable roof. She pulled out a shoe box—her treasure. In it she'd arranged a Hello Kitty coloring book, a rainbow-colored hairbrush, broken crayons, and her El Shaddai prayer hanky. All but the kerchief I'd gifted her. She said, "Anything I need is right in here."

Elma and her family let their house erode. As Elma and I watched from the terrace, and her family watched through the breakfast room's French doors, they hummed to the rhythm of the rain, collectively quelling our panic with the stillness of their Bicolano spirit. And once the entirety of the brown shanty had dissolved in the water, they proceeded with their work as if nothing was lost and the flood hadn't just consumed their home. Maximo, Elma's oldest brother and one of our "boys," fashioned a raft out of rubber tires, plywood, and my old, now-unwanted blow-up whale. He boarded his ship and smiled, then scooped utensils, a TV antenna, neon thermos cups, sunglasses, and Mama's favorite Paula Abdul workout video out of the water. Typically, he was our trash collector, gardener, and catcher of feral strays. But those "goddamn forty days," he had no task but to be captain of the sea.

Their mother, Manang Biday, also reveled in the monsoon. On sunny days she washed our clothes and linens by hand, squatted over basins and washboards in the back lot, scrubbing and kneading and wringing and sweating in the hot sun. But during the flood, she worked indoors, turning our guest-room tub into a handmade washing machine. She stood over the tub, stirring laundry into a gray-brown whirlpool with my brother's kayak paddle. She sang, "Purihin ang Panginoon." Praise the Lord. She was a queen for a day, praising the king, a queen with a batik head wrap for a crown, a kayak paddle for a scepter, and a toilet for a throne. The dark storm stood as her domain.

My father, on the other hand, drowned in threats of marital annulment, demands for repatriation of our overseas employees, bank accounts closing, ties being severed for some unpaid debt or some uncle's jealousy or some aunt's disloyalty.

"Our people are stealing from us," Mama said. "Puñeta." Mama's favorite curse word, meaning "fuck" in Tagalog, or "hand job" in street Spanish. Puñeta. Puñeta. It was the sound she constantly made while it poured and we were stuck on the main and upstairs floors, and the word that cued Papa to leave the room, to walk to the extra bedroom and to lock himself up, mapping out business plans and investment proposals and repatriation petitions until he became fatigued enough to sleep. He made calls to Saudi Arabia, Taiwan, and Hong Kong, but his efforts proved futile. I listened with my hands cupped to his door and my ear leaning against them, eavesdropping, then flinching every time he banged the receiver against the phone base.

"Hello. Hello?" he said, dialing again after being hung up on. "Please don't hang up this time. My name is Gonzalo Arcilla of Starlite Oil and the FossilFil Project. I'm looking for my men . . . Hello? Putang ina!"

I opened the door and peered in.

"Papa, are you okay?" I said.

He sat on the floor with his back against the wall and the rotary phone between his knees. "If I could just get one more person on a flight," he said, staring at the phone. "Hundreds of thousands of men and only eighty-three flights to get them home."

"Are you talking about your men, Papa? The ones stuck at war?"

He didn't answer. He didn't look at me. He just kept flipping through his Rolodex, calling people, asking questions, and praying under his breath, "God, please."

The more he tried to save our empire, the more he sank into the middle-aged man's abyss: failure, regret, and shame.

Paolo didn't play with me when it rained. He replaced me with Super Nintendo. He powered on the television and game console, blared *Street*

Fighter sounds from the speaker, and held the Nintendo control in one hand and a Pringles tube in the other—all while kicking his soccer ball onto the baseboard of his bed. The heavy clouds and lack of natural light made him a recluse. He adopted a manner of being quiet—so quiet that it sounded like a scream. I'd always known that Mama's back-and-forth between personalities was something he experienced as well; that there was a reason why he could seamlessly go from throwing tantrums and being aggressive on the soccer field to gingerly playing with a caught beetle. I always knew that there was a reason why he loved scary movies and reptile-eating reptiles and four-loop roller coasters as much as he loved plush toys. Because I loved him and had grown up with him, I understood that it took no effort for him to be the best brother, but it took every bit of his person to be a boy.

And so when Paolo refused to play or joke around with me, I found other diversions. I played *Tetris* and *Super Mario* on the Game Boy he gave to me. But when video games got old or my battery power ran out, I talked Elma into taking a dip in the water. While everyone busied themselves with chores, business plans, ledgers, cosmetics, and fashion magazines, Elma and I got in ruffled, polka-dot swimsuits—I lent her mine—and splashed around in frothy, murky water at the base of the main steps. The garden became our private pool and the red-carpeted main steps the diving board to it. I had always been a tremendous swimmer since the day Mama had thrown me into three meters of water. Mama always insisted I swim well.

I wanted Elma to swim well, too.

So I pushed her in.

She flailed her arms and slipped underneath a few times, struggling and gurgling and kicking her way up.

I yelled, "Kick up! Kick up! If you move your legs, you won't drown! Kick! C'mon! We'll prove Mama wrong!"

She kicked and thrashed her body up and almost out of the water.

I yelled again, not minding the muck floating or the baby water snakes slithering, "C'mon! Kick!"

She kicked some more.

"You can do this!"

She popped her head up, swallowed a mouthful of air, ducked under, and kicked her biggest kick. She stroked her arms forward and toward the steps, and glided almost effortlessly with her legs behind her like a mermaid's tail and her head tilted toward oxygen.

"You did it, Elma! You did it!" I reached for her hand and pulled her up to where I was sitting, wrapped my arm around her neck, touched my forehead with hers, and said, "You're not mad at me now, are you?"

She smiled and shook her head, beads of water sparkling on her face and dripping from the tips of her hair. She coughed out her words. "I can swim."

Where the hem of the water touched the edge of the mansion, Elma and I pat-a-caked and high-fived, proud of our triumph in the midst of torrential rain.

We wrapped towels around our shoulders and wore them like capes as we read at the top of the main steps. I picked out books about the ocean that day, thinking that the subject fit the weather and our being surrounded by water. The passages and pictures fueled our imagination and gave us more detail to work with for our inspired visions. Besides diving into floodwater, we pretended to wrestle giant squid, rescue sea turtles from flotsam and jetsam, and designed submarines fit for sunken-ship discovery. I read aloud to Elma, sometimes translating quotes from English to Tagalog. Some lines, some facts, however, needed no interpretation—for the ocean proclaimed truths that every ear understood.

"How far down can your submarine go, Captain?" Elma said in her sea-explorer voice.

"Down to the bottom of the Marianas, sir. Eleven kilometers to be exact," I said in mine.

"Remember to avoid those sul-*four* bubbles when you go down."

"Elma, I think it's called sul*fur* bubbles," I said.

"Right. Sul-*fur* bubbles."

"Sir, what shall I look for?"

"Oh, the usual. Prove that mermaids exist!"

"Everything—*everything*—exists in the ocean, sir! Think it up and it is there! The ocean knows everything, holds everything; it even hears everything! It keeps all our dreams and secrets!" I said.

Elma saluted. "I believe it, my friend. I mean, Captain."

After our deep-sea exploration, we pretended to be sunning at the beach, one hand as a visor and the other a rolled-up towel for a cushion between head and sand. We rolled over on our stomachs, paddling on our make-believe surfboards, ripping curls, and catching waves. Our skin smelled like sunscreen and tasted like salt. Our hair bleached in the sun. Our self-guided ocean tours led us to dolphin sanctuaries and hidden capes. We spearfished and wrestled giant squid, and before the sun's lip dipped, we dismembered octopi, one tentacle at a time. Then we turned away from the deep and imaginary navy blue and back to shore, through softer sprays of azure.

The mansion sopped in the downpour and flood. Its many gilded parts began to tarnish, including the loose threads from the decorator's tassels that thinned in the water. My parents' beautification project—investment—was now a disaster zone, no longer pretty or shiny or sweet, and most importantly, no longer a source of cash flow.

When the "goddamn forty days" were over, the water receded—it swirled into sewers and glugged, as if to say adieu, before it finally disappeared down the drain. We could, once again, see potholes. Birds could rest again on branches. The crops lay ruined. The floors at the lower level of the house remained slimy with moss and mold. Residue rested on surfaces, taking the shape of murky eddies. The flood tattooed itself on the house: waterlines to help us remember, *This is how much the storm can submerge. Never underestimate.*

The monsoon stopped and life was once more, and just once more, normal and busy. Looters took whatever of our belongings had floated through the slats in the wrought-iron gates. The boys and our maids scrubbed off the film that had slimed over all that the water touched. Mama took inventory of what remained in our possession. Papa hid in the extra bedroom, drafting and planning and making calls, and almost never came out again to steal my jacks and ball. Paolo became glued to his Nintendo, while Elma and I grew into explorers—searching unknown parts of the mansion, such as nests for birds under gables and nests for tadpoles in pocks on the driveway left by the storm. She and I also thought of exploring what was beyond—the layers of life outside the mansion's stone walls. The water made an impression on us, and we couldn't help but think of it: waterfalls, rivers, streams, lakes, and the one that called out to us—the ocean.

The sun came out from hiding, without restriction or hesitation, immediately singeing everything with its touch. It was time for us to go back to our lives, to ready both body and land, skin and soil, for the heat and burn of the scorch.

Mama, Come Back

1994

I woke up in the middle of the night to familiar sounds: the furniture creaking as it contracted in the cool air, the crickets outside, the air-conditioner humming, and my yaya snoring as two hundred pounds of her splayed on a pallet on my bedroom floor. But I woke up with a nervous feeling, a coming to, a reminder that sleeping was a lonely practice done in the dark.

Sleeping was when things changed.

My Hello Kitty night-light glowed enough to let me see what might have shifted. I looked around. Everything but one thing was where it was supposed to be. My translucent Crayola coin bank stood empty on my dresser. The peso bills I'd been given on Christmas and the Hong Kong dollar coins Papa had brought back from his travels were gone.

"Yaya! Wake up!" I said, shaking her arm.

"Mm," she said as she rolled over.

"My money's gone!" I said.

"What money?" she mumbled.

I took the coin bank from the dresser and held it up to her face. "Look!"

She rubbed her eyes and squinted and sat up in one motion. "Dali!"

I followed her as she scuffled out the doorway. She ran across the terrace and to Papa's room, while I made a pit stop at Paolo's bedside.

"Kuya!" I said. "Wake up! My money is missing!"

He opened his eyes, sat up, and slid into his slippers as if he knew exactly where my money had gone.

"Where are you going?" I asked.

"Quick!" he said, running out the door and down the steps.

Papa and Yaya stood by the master bedroom door, pursing their lips and shaking their heads.

"What?" I said.

They didn't respond.

I looked to Paolo for an explanation and all he did was grimace. He started to cry, and I did, too, although I had no idea why.

"Check the basement," Papa said to Yaya.

I then understood. I knew what the basement stood for: Mama's innermost parts. If they were checking there, it meant that they were checking for her. I knew that it was not only my coins and bills they were searching for, but my mother, who had slipped out of the mansion and into the night.

"Mama! Mama!" I cried.

I clutched my coin bank under my arm like a baby doll, and sobbed as Yaya, Paolo, and I descended down the steps. We looked inside closets and behind shelves, between armoires and under the padded bench where Mama sat to strap on her shoes. Yaya took inventory of the jewelry and Paolo looked through her clothes. When he didn't find what he was looking for, he threw hangers onto the floor.

"That's enough," Yaya said, embracing Paolo and leading him back up to the main floor. "All her things are here, so she won't be gone long."

When we emerged from Mama's cavern without her, the night had turned soggy with our sadness, as if the mansion's walls had sopped up our tears. Papa spoke on the rotary phone, asking the person on the other line about my mother's whereabouts. He thanked the person and hung up, and said to us, "Her aerobics friends don't know either."

Paolo reminded him that Mama had just purchased a cellular phone—the black block with numbered white squares. Papa flipped through the Rolodex, pulled out a card, and dialed the number written on it.

"Not answering," he said. He told Yaya to send Katring, Loring, and Elma on a search of the neighborhood, and the drivers to the nearest bus terminal. "Estrella, *why?* The kids."

"Where did she go, Papa?" I said, pulling on his sleeve.

He sat down in Mama's peacock chair and put me on his lap. "Here, help me. You read the numbers out loud and I turn the dial, okay?"

"Okay," I said. I rotated the spindle on the Rolodex and picked out a card. I read phone numbers belonging to Mama's siblings and cousins, to former clients, and to friends she had gone shopping with or had hosted for champagne or tea. With every turn of the dial, I prayed in my heart, *God, please find my mama.*

Papa began every phone conversation the same way. "Hi, yes, this is Gonzalo Arcilla. Yes, I apologize, I know my wife has aggravated you, but I hope we can set that aside for now. She's gone missing." He went on for two hours making calls. He asked whoever was on the other end of the line to pardon my mother for a named or unnamed offense. "Yes, yes, I know. I'm sorry."

The crickets still chirped outside, and the air-conditioner in the master bedroom continued to hum. Along with the night's white noise, Papa's groveling grew tedious. I started to feel sleepy. Still sitting on my father's lap, I dozed off momentarily, my chin falling to my chest. I snoozed until Papa yelled into the phone and startled me awake.

"Abra! Why the hell would she be on her way to *Abra?*" he said.

Paolo came out of the master bedroom after hours of rummaging through Mama's drawers, bags, and bins. "Abra?" he said. "But that's so far away."

Papa kept nodding as he received information over the phone. He said, "Mm-hmm. Yes, I know how far away that is. Well, thank God, she's only halfway there."

"What's Abra, Kuya?" I said.

"It's some place. She's crazy."

"Hey, don't call Mama crazy."

"She *is* crazy. Only crazy people leave their families at night and go to faraway places like Abra. I hope she falls off a cliff!"

I gasped. "That's really mean, Kuya. I hope *you* fall off a cliff!"

"Excuse me, hold on," Papa said into the phone. He held his hand over the receiver. "Stop fighting, you two. Band together, remember?"

I fell asleep in Mama's chair as Papa continued to telephone relatives and friends. Paolo slept in Mama's bed, the Game Boy resting on his chest after rounds of *Tetris*. The maids and Elma came back exhausted from searching the neighborhood on foot, and the drivers returned to the mansion without my mother.

A few hours later, we all awoke to dawn's rose-pink light and to Papa saying, "We've been looking for you. Who were you with?"

I had barely stirred to consciousness when Mama stormed into her room, escorted half-asleep Paolo out onto the long hallway, and shut the door. Papa said nothing and skulked about until he made his way to his upstairs habitation, exhausted from patrolling through the night and searching for our mother, who had, at age forty-four, lost children, lost wealth, lost health, and lost her sense of home.

Paolo kicked the master bedroom door many times, and screamed, "You left us! Papa stayed up all night looking for you!" He went into the breakfast room, picked up the Rolodex, walked back with it through the arched entryway, and hurled the spindle-card stack at Mama's door.

The cards scattered onto the floor. He bolted upstairs, screaming, "Next time, don't come back!"

But I liked that Mama came back. I liked hearing her nervous sniffs again, the jangle of her bracelets, her heels tapping against the floor, her hands whirring through her makeup organizer, and her humming. I turned the doorknob and let myself into her room, where she had undressed and left a trail of shoes and clothes. At the moment I spotted her, she was wrapping herself in her robe and tying its sash around her waist. She untucked her hair from under her collar, slipped behind a curtain, and stood there, forming a mannequin's figure behind the drapes.

Neither of us moved.

"Were you looking for me, or were you looking for your money?" she said, facing the window.

"Both," I whispered. "Where did you go, Mama? What did you do with my money?"

"Listen, I was going to give you back the cash. Stop whining already," she said.

"I want to know where you went," I said, inching forward. "I was scared."

"Scared? *Pfft*," she said in a monotone, listless and low. "You want to know what's scary? Losing everything is scary. Losing your babies, your money, your connections, your reputation, the people you thought were your friends."

I inched closer until I was an arm's length away—to hear her better and to see her. I pulled the curtain away from her, off her back, revealing what had formed next to the window, what had taken the shape and place of the mansion's matriarch, our chief of staff, our genesis. In the rose-pink light stood a woman five feet in height: a hundred pounds of sheet dress, silk robe, black hair, and the chin-up, jaw-jutted-out look of a thoroughbred. She had her hands on the windowsill, lightly, as if to play the piano. The tips of her toes grazed the baseboard. The tips of her hair came down to greasy points, tousled and unwashed. The tip of her tongue moved between her lips, her muttering inaudible and undecipherable.

I could tell she hadn't slept much. Her eyes drooped in the corners and the skin under them sagged, her lips were chapped, and her complexion was beige. She kept muttering. The only words I could make out were names: Mara, Tachio, and Mansion Royale. She kept mumbling, until finally, she snapped. "Not the mansion, too! We don't know how to be anywhere else! Puñeta!"

Her words and tone jolted me out of sadness and sympathy, and into fear. I let go of the curtain, which drifted for a moment in the air and landed on her back. The cloth confined her shakes, her mutters, her cries, and disguised her as part of the house.

She *was* part of the house. Her weeping was the mansion's very voice.

Desert of His Mind

1979

There sat on Papa's nightstand a photograph of him from before I was born. In the picture, he stood smiling next to a mustached man wearing what I called a long white dress. Papa was outfitted in linen and denim, and his hair was big, dry, and dusty. The getup and the do alone told me that the photograph was from a different time. And the hills of sand in both foreground and background stated that the photograph was from a different world.

The picture prompted stories.

They began, "I was a gardener, not a rescuer, the first time I packed my suitcases for the desert, the first time dry heat filled my nostrils with sand."

It was seven years short of the People's Revolution against Ferdinand Marcos and seven years before my existence. Papa hadn't met Mama yet, but was supporting his first wife and their two teenage children. He set off for Saudi Arabia, not hoping to build a fortune, but just to get by, to feed mouths during the peak of martial law—an era defined by the amassing of wealth by the Marcos family, the eradication of freedom of the press, and thousands of unexplained arrests, detentions, and executions without trial. Papa's own brother and childhood friends, activists, and students of history and the law protested and were many times tortured by the armed forces.

Papa also left to escape the scandal his then-wife had gotten into. She had been sleeping with Papa's closest confidante in Nueva Ecija, a logging town. The friend, the traitor, had been keeping young house-wives entertained in their village bungalows while the husbands hiked up the mountain for work. One day, instead of chopping down a tree, one of the village husbands took his bolo knife and hacked the town lover to death. Every man with a wife became suspect. Shamed for being a cuckold and swarmed by gossip about a crime, Papa fled the mountains and forest, his natural habitat. At first, he wanted distance, not fortune nor heroism nor acclaim.

He left his wife and two teenage children, a girl and a boy, whom he would send money to for a decade. Papa did not see his first daughter and son until after I was born. He invited them to my birthday parties, including the one when I stole licks of icing from the cake, when the night robbed us of our baby brother.

Papa's children had grown up with barely anything, but they made it to Metro Manila, and both graduated from university, married, and became entrepreneurs. When my parents first moved into the mansion, Mama gave them permission to visit, but soon after the Gulf War, per Mama's judgment, they were once again estranged.

At the time, Papa was an agricultural engineer with a knack for entrepreneurship and for leading men. He had just spent nearly a decade as a logger in the mountains of the Sierra Madre. Just six days after Papa hiked down the cordillera, a man—a lawyer, a genie, an adviser to the prince—found him filling out forms at a recruitment agency in Manila. Reading the transcript from over Papa's shoulder, the man in a thawb—an ankle-length, white robe-like garment—and a red-and-white-checked headdress offered Papa what the man called "a special job."

"My name is Ahmed Al-Ajmi," the man said. "Can you help me? I'm under time pressure for a special project."

"Sir?"

"You know about plants and trees, yes?"

"Yes, sir. I am a logger. I just came down from working on the Sierra Madre."

"Good, good. You know about people, yes?"

"I lead a group of men on the sierra, sir."

"Good, good. So you can help me, yes, Mohandes?"

"Sir?"

"Mohandes. Engineer, builder, fixer."

"I see. Where and when, sir?"

"We leave for the Royal Kingdom of Saudi Arabia tomorrow, Mohandes."

"Tomorrow, sir?"

"Yes, I am under time pressure, you see. Tomorrow, yes, Mohandes?"

"Will I have time to pack, sir? What should I bring?"

"Nothing, Mohandes. Everything will be provided. Everything."

The next day, Papa arrived in Saudi Arabia by jet, where Ahmed Al-Ajmi welcomed him with a handshake and a kiss on the cheek. They were now close friends. Al-Ajmi asked about his plane ride, his children, and his health, but never the topic of wives. He led Papa to a 1979 Land Rover, which drove through dust lands for hours, through desert and more desert, past ancient Riyadh mud-house relics and a souk—a market where animals, imported produce, and spices were traded by bargaining. It was while driving past this souk that Papa first understood man-woman relations in the Middle East. He saw men purchasing goats and sheep, dragging the mammals by their bound legs, and throwing them into the back seat of a luxury American or European car, crammed next to one or two or three wives. The wives wore coverings from temple to toe, and never looked their husbands or other men (including Papa) in the eye. Papa became certain that he no longer was in Nueva Ecija or Manila.

At a stop, Al-Ajmi gestured for Papa to exit the vehicle, to which Papa reacted with a smile and a quick unbuckling of his seat belt, as he had needed to use the bathroom since landing. As Papa walked around the vehicle in search of a spot where he could relieve himself, the royal adviser beckoned Papa to stand with him on a sand hill.

"What do you think of the place, Mohandes?"

"This place, sir? You mean the desert?"

"You believe it can be a good site for a project?"

"It depends on what kind of project, sir."

"Mohandes, you are to do something no one has done before. You are to build a greenhouse—the first greenhouse in the Arabian Desert."

"A greenhouse?" Papa said, scratching his head and scanning the rolls and hills and dips and kilometers of sand around him. "Good god, a greenhouse."

Papa knelt down, forked his fingers into the warm powder, scooped up a sample, and examined the specimen he was ordered to tame. In his hand, he had a fistful of dust, of ashes that formed an ancient royal kingdom—a kingdom controlling the entry and exit, the digging and exchanging, the exporting and withholding of oil. In his hand, he held mighty microbes that once belonged to Bedouins, sons and brothers and cousins, wanderers belonging to nothing but caravans, the scarcity of water, and the waywardness of the wind.

There must be a reason why the Bedouins never settled, Papa thought. *This is an impossible place to live, to build.* Then again, studying the particles in his hand, sifting them through his wrinkled fingers, he found bits, dots, a peppering of hope: soil hiding in sand.

"Sir, if you bring me soil, I will plant you a garden."

Papa spent the evening drafting plans to modernize agriculture in the Middle East and praying under his breath for a miracle in barren land. He slept in his camp house not knowing what was to arrive in the morning. In the land where sinking air motioned you to slumber, and scorched skin and a parched throat woke you up in the morning, Papa woke to clouds of dust and smoke rising and puffing from a convoy of trucks, bulldozers, drillers, graders, and forklifts. Al-Ajmi was adviser not only to a family who yearned for Arabian-grown vegetables, but who also owned distributorships for Japanese construction equipment and Dutch supplies.

"Mohandes, while you were sleeping, these arrived from Narita and Rotterdam."

"But . . ."

"But you thought, Mohandes, it was impossible. Let me tell you, my friend, with Saudi Arabians, nothing is impossible. Nothing."

Papa spent his first two weeks overseeing the construction of workers' barracks, ordering air-conditioners, utensils, bedding, and toiletries from Al-Ajmi's office. It was then that Al-Ajmi introduced him to Abdullah, the Egyptian foreman who'd been on-site for several years. Abdullah had been supervising the hundreds of Egyptian and Pakistani workers hired for other projects, and he was now to partner with Papa in making room for Filipino workers. A Filipino who had been driving Papa around from site to site tipped him off about the animosity that once existed between the Egyptian and Pakistani workers, and the new tension now felt because of the expected arrival of Southeast Asian logging and farming men. Abdullah declined to shake Papa's hand and cut his introduction short to "Here is where we eat and there is where we sleep. I am in charge."

Papa allocated the third week for hiring men from Nueva Ecija— loggers he had met on the sierra, rice farmers from the Maligaya Rice Research and Training Center, and low-paid professors from Central Luzon State University, an agricultural college. He recruited men who knew the nature of foliage and flora, men who could give life to plants with their gardening hands, who could direct a vine to turn up or bend down, but could never satisfy the yearnings of a wife for heft in the bank and ardor in bed. He uprooted them from the rice fields and blue mountains, and brought them to the Middle East for a promise: that for every shrub they kept alive, for every crate of produce harvested, they each could pocket more than their wives could ever ask. Thousands signed up and boarded planes. Papa's first venture at being an enlister convinced him that one day, recruitment would be a more-than-viable source of income. Saudi Arabia and its neighbors had dreams bigger than the subcontinent, but a population of princes reluctant to do manual labor. And there it was—Papa's gold mine: a wealthy state eager to hand out employment to whoever was willing to break their backs and scald their skin for the expansion of an empire.

When the first wave of workers flew in from Manila, Papa proved to them and to Abdullah that he was there to protect and serve his men. Abdullah had instructed the cook, his Egyptian ally, to feed hard-boiled eggs and rock-hard dried fish solely to Filipino and Pakistani workers. After a week, the workers took to protest and asked Papa to act upon the issue. So he acquired a written consent from Al-Ajmi, saying that Abdullah ranked lower than Papa, and that he was to hire two additional cooks—one Pakistani and one Filipino—to make varieties that reminded the workers of the sweet, spicy, savory tastes of home. Papa took on the task of going to market so that Abdullah and his cook couldn't pinch away a portion of the stipend for themselves. Mohandes wanted to care for and protect his men through and through.

One afternoon, Papa and his driver went to the souk for items requested by the three cooks. He bagged kilo after kilo of fruits, nuts, and grains, bargaining with the merchant and winning him over with his stories. In mid-conversation, loud calls came from speakers and horns. Men purchasing halal foods turned to one direction, knelt down, and prayed. Papa—a first-timer in a Muslim land and a Catholic by heart and heritage, unaware of the forbiddance of human activity at such a moment— kept bagging crops into woven sacks. Before the merchant could warn or instruct him, a mutawa—a religious policeman—struck Papa with a leather cord and flogged him until he fell to the ground. The driver waited for a pause in the beating, pulled Papa by the arm, and carried him off to the freight truck without any of their bags of sundries. For over a week, Papa slept on his stomach and worked under the Arabian sky, bleeding through the cloth on his back.

Nevertheless, he pushed through with plans: leveled the rolling hills of sand with diggers and bulldozers, built a foundation with a cork-and-wood subfloor tilted at forty-five degrees for gravity-led irrigation, dug a well, and devised a cooling and misting system out of insulated pipes—a system that recycled the little amount of water they had. He imported nutrient-rich soil from the Philippines and moisture-retaining peat moss from Holland, and sprinkled them onto a kilometer-wide square, and fashioned panels of glass around the new earth: a prism that collected light and a tank that bottled up moisture—a flower and vegetable garden in the middle of the Arabian Desert, the expanse known to have scorched throats, charred bones, and swallowed up creeping and crawling creatures.

The greenhouse had two primary purposes: first, to stand and gleam under the sun, for all men and wives to see just how majestic, how powerful, how wealthy Al-Ajmi's superiors were; and, second, to produce the coolest, most refreshing of trellised vines—cucumber.

"The Americans, they put the cucumber on their eyes to cool them. And they pickle them and eat them in the summertime," Al-Ajmi said. "We want cucumbers here, Mohandes. We are tired of importing these small, refreshing squashes. We want to wow the world, my friend. Just imagine, cucumbers growing in the desert."

Papa's commitment to his crops became a devotion. He played priest, an intermediary between the celestial and the vegetal, begging God to give just enough sun and just enough water, and whispering to the plants, "Hush. Drink. Feed. Grow. Hush." He instructed his men to be like parishioners, daily attending what could have been Mass—a holy sacrifice of till, tears, and sweat; a series of sacraments: the mulching of soil, the deep watering of roots, the dressing with compost, the trimming of weeds, the fervent supplication for seeds to fall on good soil, and the veiling of crops from the high sun. Each sixty-four-day cycle culminated with a Eucharistic rite, a celebration of the yield, a breaking—not of bread—but of cool, crunchy Holland Hothouse bitter-free cucumber, announcing, "Hallelujah! The harvest is here!"

At night, when the Egyptians, Pakistanis, and Arabs left for their tents, Papa and his men from the cordillera circled around the fire, wrapped in sunset-colored blankets woven by the Bedouins. Each shared a story of survival or confessed a sin: one man escaped from prison, another escaped a town fire. Papa admitted to having missed his family, but declared praises to God for having brought him out of Nueva Ecija, and away from his childhood spent half on the street and half in the fish market. He talked about his two children and about starting over again. He mentioned dreams of a new chapter in Manila, in the big city, possibly with a new woman, an educated, sophisticated one, and building a life—an empire—so very non-provincial, so worldly, so classy, so metropolitan, so sparkling, so divine.

Papa and his men toasted tin cups—an amen to a brother—and let moonlight reflect on their dust-covered, tear-filled eyes. At each day's end, they circled together, orbiting a fire that kept them warm and scared off creatures of the dark. The fire became like Moses's burning bush, a beckoning toward rest and a calling to mission. Their nightly fireside circle became church for them—a congregation of Catholic dropouts in Muslim-Arab land. Papa built not only a greenhouse in the desert but a parish on sand hills.

Papa, the gardener, the grower, the nurturer. Papa, the maker. Papa, the friend. Papa, the engineer and designer, the leader, the magician. In the desert, Papa became like many of the stars he watched at night: Leo, the Lion; Orion, the Hunter; and Perseus, the Hero.

Each night, after he put out the fire and before the badlands turned too cold, Papa lay on the sand and looked up. He made dusk a cathedral, and the sky a painting on the basilica's ceiling. He pointed at constellations and named new ones, and read from them parables for the desert wanderer. "Thank you," he called out to the brilliance above. And right there, where the Bedouins had roamed, where many had drifted, and where the world's religions were born, the brilliance confirmed in Papa's heart, with a sparkling and a glinting and a quiet that echoed the breathing of God, "This is your place."

1985

Cactus and orchid danced.

He, a recruiter and oil importer, and she, a doctor and pageant queen, do-si-doed in the hallway connecting their two offices. In his wing of the prime commercial complex, he signed work contracts and traded engine lubricant. On hers, she took heart rates, recorded blood pressure, and prescribed medicine.

The cactus—a product of the sun, dark from Indio birth and tan from recent travels to Kuwait—spoke with a voice reverberating from a body that once had braved something impossible, something far from home, something desperate and hot.

The orchid—fragrant, soft in her white pantsuit, yet striking from the tip of her mestiza nose to the tip of her lacquered finger—possessed a confidence so sharp, it cut through the flirting space between them.

"Estrella of LVM Medical Centre," she said, "and you?"

"Gonzalo of Orion Recruitment and Starlite Oil," he replied.

Just a year later, I was born.

They bought a house together—a mansion on the foot of the Antipolo hill. It had ten bedrooms, a sprawling lawn, a meandering driveway, a ballroom, a disco hall, a breakfast room and dining room, a basement for a closet, and two terraces hanging over a rice paddy and a convent.

The monsoon frequented the mansion. The monsoon washed it throughout and through-in. The orchid lost her license for having issued more health certificates than she had performed medical exams. And the cactus lost thousands of men to dust storms and the war between Uncle Sam and Saddam Hussein.

The monsoon let the orchid live.

The monsoon nearly killed the cactus; it could only survive by replanting itself in the sand.

1994

A constellation of sparks dotted the Arabian Desert at night—eyes watching, waiting. Eyes that could have belonged to wolves, sand cats, and striped hyenas adapted to waterless living. These sparks, however, flickered not from the faces of mammals bred for arid areas, but from the faces of men promised employment in Saudi Arabia, Jordan, Kuwait, the Emirates, and Qatar—the seeds to my parents' fortune. Papa recruited them from 1979 through 1990, adding their names to a ledger of Filipino workers venturing abroad. For every laborer sent to the Middle East, Papa received a fee. For every work contract signed, Mama gave a medical exam and issued a health certificate required for a visa. Together, my parents operated a machine that simultaneously drained the Philippines of under- and unemployed men, and fed the Crescent and the Gulf with the labor force it needed to develop and dig. My parents acted as middlemen between princes and paupers, a rising empire and a failing one. They brought thousands upon thousands from the islands, only to be caught in the First Gulf War, only to be left with the responsibility of bringing each one of the workers home.

The Gulf War lasted from mid-1990 through early 1991, but the effects on Filipino-Arab relations continued. In 1994, soon after my eighth birthday, Papa talked about his men meandering—shoeless, hungry, thirsty, and delirious. He talked about having to save them, having to bring them back home. *Every single one.* He talked about those who had died, but mostly, he talked about those who survived. He talked about how strong they were, how they had scrounged for food, evaded checkpoints, ran from rebel soldiers, spotted relief workers and journalists, found camps, found telephones, found water.

"They stay alive because they know I will rescue them and bring them back home, and find them jobs here," Papa said. "If I stay in the mansion, I will die. And if I die, they die."

The desert in Papa's mind: sand dunes, dry air, blistered knuckles, chapped lips, pet goats for company and for slaughter, and sweaty, dust-flecked brows belonging to thirsty men. These men walked through the Arabian Desert for weeks, maybe months, but really years, and most of them lost track of the whereabouts of home. Some of their friends now lay past scorch and in decay, buried not under fertile soil, but dull gray-black stones, in unnamed graves spotting the badlands. The living ones wandered, dressed in tatters, with shreds of their dead comrades' clothing as turbans, night and day, hoping both to be rescued and to remain unfound. They were men who'd worked for years in a greenhouse, an oil field, or in an oil tycoon's palace, and now left undocumented and unemployed because of the Gulf War. They entrusted their lives to my parents with a sign of their names on a dotted line, for the promise of employment in Abraham's many nations: Saudi Arabia, Jordan, Kuwait, the Emirates, and Qatar. They were men who prayed to God, but belonged to Papa. God Almighty their Provider, but Papa their Savior.

And he knew this. He believed it.

Which is why when he emptied a cup of coffee in one steady sip at breakfast, he stared out into the distance, or why the picture on his nightstand made him cry, or why he fell silent at my bedside while singing "You Are My sunshine." He heard his workers' pleas; he felt the sweat of their brows on his brow.

Papa had built a multinational business with the flex of these men's muscles, with the tendons that connected not just tissue to bone, but the indulgence of the Arab world with the diligence of the Filipino workforce and the American need—or greed—for oil. He recruited them primarily as aides in building the first greenhouse in the desert, and thereafter as workhands wherever his Arab partners needed laborers, an oil site, a car lubricant–packaging plant, a five-star hotel, a would-be international city that later became known as Dubai.

Gonzalo Arcilla: self-made family man, survivor of Third World poverty, storyteller, and nexus between America, Arabia, and our seven-thousand-island archipelago.

As I ran up the driveway from a day of playing with Elma, two suitcases at the top of the stairs stopped me in my tracks. Papa stood next to the luggage, a corner of his prized photograph peeking out from a half-zipped suitcase pocket. He knelt down and cupped my cheeks in his hands, and said, "I have to go. I have to see to my men."

He said he couldn't repatriate his ten thousand workers if he didn't leave the mansion, and that staying would mean the death of him. He said all his efforts to salvage the mansion had failed, that there was no redeeming their marriage, that Mama now loved another man. He said his plan was to find another livelihood and to start anew, to gather funds so he could buy his men plane tickets home. Then he would come for Paolo and me.

He had every good reason to leave. But what he saw when he looked out into the distance, I couldn't see. All I saw were two suitcases, one medium and one small, but both large enough to fit me in with the clothes and compasses and water jugs and dreams and visions he had packed to take with him.

Papa had to save the world he had built, but first he had to leave.

He folded me into his arms and I felt the heat of Arabia emanate from deep within him. He gripped the hair on the back of my head with one hand and the back side of my collar with the other. His chin and the hard bite on his lower lip shuddered on my shoulder, and mine on his. We cried into each other, with eyes shut, making sounds only sad mammals made, my tears mixing with his tears in beads of sorrow collecting on our sleeves. The wet spots were the water he took with him to the desert; the last bit of moisture he salted away from the flood.

We held on and held on. We kept holding on until the wind breezed by and signaled that it was time for him to leave.

He let go, first of my hair and collar, and then of the rest of the child that was me. I swallowed my spit, and felt it slide down, then clog my throat. Unable to move, unable to speak, I hurt in places outside my body. I told myself to hurt more because, perhaps, my aching would be stronger than the sun. Perhaps a daughter with curled fists, digging her nails into her palms, could show the man with packed suitcases that he was hurting me as only a father could hurt his child.

"Promise me, you'll always remember, none of this is normal. But we were not made for normal, and for that, I am sorry, my warrior girl," Papa said. "Be brave, be smart, be kind, and have faith. Remember that you are made of light."

He turned away and slipped into the light and space before him, and disappeared out of the mansion's landscape and into the desert of his mind.

PART TWO

PART TWO

Elvis Face

The mansion was supposed to be my parents' masterpiece: the Antipolo hill as the easel, the stone walls as the canvas, and the people its every hue. But the last tad of inspiration left that midweek when, after I had been playing with Elma in the back lot all morning, I sensed that the house had received its unwanted visitor. At nine years old, I had the curiosity of a kindergartner and the questioning of a teen. Papa left some six months ago, and now, the wind, the geist, the stale smell wafting in the ether, told me that the man who sang me into sunshine was being replaced.

There lived in my mind things I was aware of but failed to understand: Tachio's death; the struggle for Paolo to be a boy; the disappearance of all things big, bright, and beautiful; and alta sociedad Mama, Indio Papa, and the span between. And now, I gained awareness of another.

This other tracked the main steps with shoe prints larger than I had ever seen before. The prints came to a square tip, unlike the leather pairs with rounded toes that Papa wore. I stepped into one of the sole-shaped marks and fit both feet heel-to-toe in the length of this person's shoe. I tiptoed out of it, this gray-black impression that at smeared parts resembled pocks in an ogre's face. I walked farther up the steps, only to find two suitcases—one large and one extra-large, both tagged with the letters EWR>MNL, Newark to Manila.

The main doors parted, the doorknobs warm, the gold-plated keyhole scratched at the mouth, as if someone, after much jingling, fumbling, and forcing, had penetrated it with a newcomer's key. I pushed open the right-side door and slipped through, making no sound except for my shallow breathing.

Kuya, where are you? I kept thinking as I edged along from doorway to hallway. The walls rumbled with the clamor coming from the breakfast room, but I approached the prattle anyway. Papa's last words to me included a command to be brave. So there I was, taking heed. The closer I came to the breakfast room, the stronger the smell of Anaïs Anaïs became, signaling that Mama, along with the square-toed, big-footed visitor who'd muddied our marble and terra-cotta floors, occupied the space where I once listened to her closed-lip singing, where I once breathed in her softness.

The arched entryway gave space to tarry, my back against the wall—a pit stop between life then and life now. *Who is Mama with?* I wondered. *A man*, I answered, hearing the baritone. *An American*, I added as I deciphered the accent—long *o*'s, open *u*'s, soft *f*s. Curiosity wouldn't leave me be, so one foot after another, I walked into their space and saw what life at the mansion was becoming—what it would become.

"Is this her?" the man said. "The smart one who writes and draws?"

"That's her," Mama said, sniffing. "She's gifted and will make me rich again one day."

"Is that so?" the man said as he reached to shake my hand. "Norman."

I pulled my hand away.

"Strong will, this one. I like it," he said. "We're gonna have fun, little miss." He stirred sweetener into his coffee, took a sip, and quickly spat it out. "Nasty! You Filipinos don't know how to make coffee! You call this 'coffee,' this *instant* stuff? First thing tomorrow, we're buying a coffeemaker."

He rattled on, sitting in my mother's rattan peacock chair, talking about his upbringing in Abra, his laundrywoman mother, and his American father. He listed micro and macro changes he would spearhead. "We don't need maids, just the laundrywoman. Keep her—she's the lowest-paid one, plus she has those children we can use. They come as a package, don't they? Sell the last sedan; keep the van and the Land Cruiser. There's so much space in this goddamn house, we better make use of it. Make money. We'll turn that back lot into a moneymaker. And golly, rice porridge for breakfast? Donuts! We're eating donuts from now on. That's how the big boys do it in Jersey. Donuts and real coffee."

"Lorna!" Mama called out to Yaya. "Call a meeting for the maids tonight."

Norman rattled and prattled, and I tuned him out. My ears fought to hear life outside: the singing nuns, the wind blowing through the rice paddy, the jeering between Elma and her siblings. And Mama? I barely recognized her. She sat in Papa's old chair, cocking her head back with a fast laugh—her every response to the man's every word. She had never been a pleaser, never known to tease, or hoot, or, really, take orders or suggestions from another. She ignored her soft-steeped tea, when I had never seen her wait for her morning drink to get cold. I had seen Mama wear her Chanel pantsuit accessorized with a raised brow, a high tone, or a bad word. But never ever, not in the years I had lived in that ten-bedroom house, had I seen the suit paired with an eagerness to gratify another.

Why him?

I studied his moves. He cleaned his teeth with his tongue, clicking it to remove the food stuck between. He clenched the ends of his armrests while talking and slapped his knees to punctuate his lines. He tossed his keys—*our keys*—from hand to hand, as if readying to pitch. He never stopped moving, didn't carry the ease Papa had when carrying conversation. His many mannerisms outnumbered Papa's. In fact, Papa only had one—his only gesture was to embrace us.

So why him?

My eyes traveled and landed on his face, his Elvis face—a mass of forehead, low-riding eyelids, prominent cheekbones with full and droopy cheeks, a broad jaw, a small mouth curling to one side, and a cleft chin. He sat there, bashing our coffee and porridge, and obstructing breakfast—my most favorite time of the day—with his unkind words, raised brow, Hollywood smile, and dimpled nose from where all his facial components measured their symmetry.

That's it! His nose—his narrow, high-bridged nose. It matched that of Mama's, of Tachio's, of Our Lady's. And his skin buffed within the same shade range as theirs. I watched him and Mama fall into each other's wanting, nod along to each other's plans. When I couldn't take a minute more, I closed my eyes, and, as I had the habit of doing in that room, breathed Mama in. I smelled a lingering of Anaïs Anaïs, but with a trace of sweat—the kind that had been trapped long enough, and finally released as vapor from right under, an impenetrable film of product and pride. I took the mix of scents as a chemosignal from the air.

Be smart, Papa told me the last time I saw him, the last time we embraced. I took his words as this: I needed to use not only my head but my gut and my senses to interpret a situation, a person, or a place. Our world, our country, our home was in some kind of war, I remembered. And sniffing out the Common Enemy ranked first on my list of duties.

Him.

He sweated through his short-sleeve button-down, unaccustomed to Manila heat. The mansion was down to two air-conditioners: one in the master bedroom and another in Paolo's room.

Norman, the big mouth, patted off his perspiration with our table linens. His sweaty Elvis face glared and signaled to me, like a flare missiled to the sky, that a battleground now lay within our stone walls. *The Common Enemy. Whatever it is that makes us unhappy.*

"Been living in America for three decades. I forget how hot it is here. Golly, *ooph*, hot like hell," he said. "Estrella, love, have the maids fetch more ice water, then fire them."

Mama leaned over for a kiss and said, "I'll take care of those ignorant ingrates tonight."

"All part of the plan," he said.

"You know me, love. I come from power; I will stay in power," she said. "Benny bonita." She smiled the smile of the little girl from the sepia pictures.

They continued saying things that I thought people only said in the movies or were taglines for Paolo's video games. They talked about being in office, expanding the mansion, going to hotels, and meeting with investors. They alternated whispering with yelling, him with his wheeze-laugh, and her with her humming.

The oddness, the newness, the veering away from what had been— they made me slide down a fork from the breakfast table and into the slip of yesteryear's now-outgrown petticoat skirt.

Jeepney Joyride

1996

"I hate that motherfucker," Paolo said as he punched the wall. "He's fired everyone. He's taken away everything. Fuck him!"

"Kuya, don't curse. It scares me," I said, pulling him away from the wall and toward the bed. We sat on the edge, my short ten-year-old legs dangling off the side and his fifteen-year-old feet planted firm and heavy, as if to funnel all his anger into the hardwood floor. He kept cracking his knuckles, grunting, grinding his teeth so hard that I could hear the enamel crush into dust.

We hadn't eaten more than one-and-a-half meals a day for the past three weeks. Mama said it was all she could afford, and Norman wasn't spending any more money on us because he had to feed his chickens. When we ate, it was a mound of rice for each of us and a can of sardine or tuna to share. The rice was hot, the viand cold and oily. I never complained about not having three square meals a day because I knew it could've been worse—but Paolo had had it. It was getting to him. He'd been cutting classes to look for food money, borrowing from friends, or selling what he called "things." When he didn't find enough cash to buy both of us lunch, he'd buy a cigarette and a stick of gum. Smoking kept his hunger satisfied and sugar kept me going.

Sometimes I thought of cutting class, too. I'd grown tired of lying to the lunch lady, making up excuses for not having cash that day. "I forgot my wallet," I said on Monday. "Do you guys have change for five hundred pesos? Oh, you don't. I'll break the bill after school and pay you tomorrow," I said on Tuesday. "You know what, I used up that five hundred pesos at the bookstore yesterday. Can you just add this to my credit?" I said on Wednesday. By Thursday there was no use even walking up to the lunch line. The lunch lady had her eyes fixed on me since I walked into the canteen, like she'd figured out my scam.

I had nice friends who wanted to lend me money, but I didn't want to borrow so often that they'd find out I'd never be able to pay them back. I didn't want to take on loan after loan from my school friends, blowing my cover and revealing to the elite student body that I was, in fact, poor. Mama said that we had nothing left—no money in the bank and no bank to trust us with a credit line. All we had to our name was the mansion and our place in Manila high society, and that place I had to help secure.

Papa never made it to the Middle East. Travel authorities and finances wouldn't allow it—restrictions that demoted his plans from saving *the* world to saving *our* world. He set up a business consultancy at the Quezon City Parks and Wildlife Circle with a folding table and a camping chair, leftover yellow pads from the recruitment agency, a can of pencils as a paperweight, a framed picture of me and Paolo, a typewriter that he typed on with his two index fingers, a stapler, and a sign that said, "Got ideas? I got business plans." Passersby often ignored him and sometimes hooted. On occasion, tree monkeys visited him, begging for crumbs of his Fita biscuits. Once or twice a week, a pedestrian stopped at his table to pitch an idea: pre-cured and prepackaged alligator meat, cane juice concentrate, foil-wrapped roasted chestnuts, street food carts—businesses for lower-middle- to lower-class entrepreneurs. He collected little to no consulting fees, feeling bad for charging men and women who, like him, scraped to get by.

When he did make a profit, he snuck into my school to give me money. Mama and Norman had forbidden Papa from coming to the mansion or, really, seeing us. Being the naturally congenial person that he was, Papa befriended the security guards at school and told them stories until they finally let him in. Whatever he had he gave to me, sacrificing his own meals for mine. But soon he saw us less frequently because he needed the time to find other sources of income: office work for past business partners, direct selling, cooperative-funded research on fishing technology, and nutritional product demonstrations. Paolo and I stretched the cash Papa sent us as far as we could, buying nearly expired peanut butter and bottom-shelf ramen noodles from the sari-sari, a kiosk selling newspapers, tabloids, and sundries. But it quickly ran out.

"I got this," Paolo said. "Don't worry about telling Papa. He doesn't need to know this—he's out there trying, too. I got this."

We thought of ways to make money while not giving away our secret—that we were two hungry kids living in a formerly opulent, now beggarly mansion run by a mother and her lover who sold fake deeds and nonexistent property, and licked the boots of politicians up north and sheriffs down in the capital. While Mama and Norman caroused through the city on their day-to-day gamble, Paolo and I stared at the ceiling, exchanging jokes and smoking invisible cigarettes.

I rolled off the bed and rummaged through Paolo's trundle drawers, searching for items we could pawn or sell. All that the drawers contained were miscellanies from our nineties childhood: plastic we slapped onto our wrists, plastic that melted into moldable goop, and plastic that grew in the water. I moved on to my bedroom, looking for anything with resale value, or anything that could remind me of an employable skill I possessed, but to no avail. Paolo searched his room as well, looking inside closets and chests.

"I got it!" Paolo said, sprinting from his room to mine. He held an army green G.I. Joe jeep in the hand he had just punched the wall with. "A jeepney!"

"Like the trucks I used to ride with Yaya?" I asked.

"They're not trucks," he said, now crouched down and zooming his jeep forward and back on the floor. "They're jeeps left behind by American soldiers. Filipino drivers painted and decorated them, and turned them into colorful rides."

"Yeah, but we don't own a jeep."

He'd been driving both of us to school since Norman clubbed and fired the last driver. Norman claimed that we were a bunch of worthless, idle Manila brats who could do a thing or two for society. So he sold Papa's Mitsubishi Lancer and got us a honky-tonk L300 van with a steering wheel wrapped in duct tape.

"But I have a van and I own music," Paolo said.

I liked the idea. We had all that we needed: Paolo's driver's license and my creativity. We dashed to the car lot and washed the van with buckets and rags Maximo had left on the terrace. We beat and rinsed the floor mats, wiped the dashboard, and polished the leather stick shift and knobs.

"I found us a barker," Paolo said, sliding his car keys across the table.

"A what?" I said, catching the keys and twirling them by the chain around my finger.

"A barker. You know, the person who rallies passengers together before a route," he said.

"I know what a barker is. I've seen them when Papa or Yaya used to take me on joyrides. But what do we need one for?"

"For the plan," he said. "We're gonna make us some money, you'll see."

That week Paolo introduced me to a senior at his school: Jordan. He was long and thin and talked with the raspy, high-pitched voice of a lady smoker. When he introduced himself to me, he did it with a curtsy and a tip of his baseball cap, his voice scraping out of his throat with a breath of heavy nicotine: "Ahhht hhyourrchh sehhhrrrvice, mahh-dhaam." Then he held his hand up for a high five and gave me a lollipop. I warmed to him right away, as if I could tell that he liked kids and kids liked him. That, and the fact that he seemed as needy as we were. He looked hungry, too.

"We're gonna be business partners, us three," he said, while clearing his throat. "I'll be the barker, Paolo will be the driver, and most importantly, you'll be the conductor in charge of collecting fares and keeping order in the van." He coughed twice.

"Me?" I said in disbelief. "*I* get to do that?"

Paolo figured out that we weren't the only starving kids in our elite schools. By observation (a skill he got from Papa) and interrogation (a skill he got from Mama), he sniffed out all the other pretenders at both of our prestigious all-girls and all-boys schools. We negotiated fixed rates and arranged regular routes, making air-conditioning and all-you-want hip-hop radio our selling point. Jordan stressed that our van was cleaner and cheaper than any public or private school bus service in the city, and I pointed out that riding in a gray van with other upper-class kids was much less humiliating than taking the commoner's colorful jeepney.

"Who would you rather be caught riding in a vehicle with, us or a bunch of janitors and secretaries?" I said.

We became a hit. Sometimes the van overflowed with so many students that we'd have to make two trips before school and two trips after. We charged each kid twenty pesos each way, enough to buy a stick of chicken barbecue—not the feet or a beak, but thighs and a breast—and a cup of rice. The van fit ten people plus us three amigos, making us two hundred yummy, crunchy, oh-so-good pesos each time on the route. We made enough for three meals, a few sticks of menthols, and a fat wad of the sweetest, juiciest, pinkest gum. Sometimes we bought mixtapes, too, to keep up our reputation as the "cool hip-hop van."

We had all sorts of kids on the van. There was the chubby, sticky goalkeeper who foamed at the mouth, the heartthrob whose parents got divorced and got back together and got divorced again, the math whiz who wanted to run for student body president but couldn't afford campaign posters, the boy sent from California so he could "learn how people lived in the Third World," the ex-congressman's son and daughter who had to hide from the media after their father's scandal, the only child who had a car but preferred to commute to and from school with company, and the guy who was there "mainly for the music."

Our second week in business, we baptized one another with new names.

Paolo put the key in the ignition once everyone got situated in the back and turned around from the driver's seat, held out a stack of mixtapes, and said, "Place your hands on the tapes and repeat after me."

We all reached forward for the tapes, some of us hunched over the kid in front, and repeated after him. "By the power vested in me by Biggie, I pledge allegiance to the cool hip-hop van. And in the spirit of brotherhood, I swear to keep everyone's secrets, and I rename the person to my left."

Paolo turned to Jordan, who was riding shotgun, and said, "Since I'm the captain, I'll go first. I name you 'Barker.'" He faked a cough.

We all laughed.

"All right, all right," Jordan said, holding his index finger against his lips. He pointed the same finger at the goalkeeper. "I name you 'Frenchie,' because all you talk about is French-kissing girls."

Each of us took a turn at being funny and clever, bestowing a nom de guerre on a friend.

Frenchie followed. "I name you 'Cheat-ah,' because you cheat on your exams. I've seen you roll up pieces of paper with algebra formulas into your pen's stem. You're brilliant, man, but you are a cheater." He high-fived the math whiz, who shook his head while snickering.

"Okay, okay," Cheat-ah said. "I name this schoolboy right here 'Westie,' for his unfailing love for West Coast hip-hop . . . even though we all know that Brooklyn and the Bronx make better music!"

We all *ooooooh*ed.

"Easy now. Have some respect for my San Diego roots," the boy from California responded. "Now, you, little one. What should we call you?"

"Beaver teeth?" I said, remembering a name I'd been called before because of my protruding front teeth.

"Nah," he said, taking a pen from his polo shirt's pocket. He took my Lucky Star hand and doodled on it. "Prinsesa."

They all *ooooooh*ed again, and I blushed.

Paolo saw how embarrassed I was. He interjected, "Okay, kiddos. I think that's it for today. DJ Paolo has some fresh tunes for us this afternoon." He pushed the cassette into the deck and pressed "Play," then adjusted his rearview mirror and made eye contact with me. He smiled at me with his eyes, to which I responded by sticking out my tongue.

The kids in the van sang loud and banged their heads to music our mothers and Catholic schoolteachers would never have approved of. We passed around teen magazines stolen from the coffee shop or library. We took jabs at slam poetry—original tracks that we were convinced Dr. Dre and LL Cool J would be proud of. We took naps and farted on each other, turning the van into a venue for practical jokes. We helped one another with our homework, and talked about the things we loved and loathed, and all the dreams we each had.

"I want to be a writer," I said each time.

"Then go be a writer, little girl," they would all say in between puffs of joints or cigarettes. I loved those kids and that van. And the best part was, they loved me back.

Paolo and I cleaned the van with Elma on Sunday afternoons when her mother didn't ask her to help with laundry. She taught us how to clean the windshield free of streaks and how to beat the car mats with a broken broom. Paolo introduced her to music she liked to call "tunog Amerika." American sound.

"Like this," Elma said, showing me how to make figure eights with the swish of a rag. She reminded me of Katring and Loring, and of how much I missed them.

"I'm doing it, look! Kuya, look! I can do the figure eights!" I said.

"Ha, maybe you were born to be a maid, who knows?" Paolo said, jeering.

"Maybe," I said, slapping my rag over my shoulder. "I wouldn't mind it at all."

We washed our joyride with the same kind of delight we got from watching the debutantes dance on the main floor. The van became a new place for us to gather, to sing, to play.

But sometimes the van failed us. When it was too hot, it broke down. When it was too rainy, it wouldn't start at all. When it was too packed, we would get pulled over for charges of overloading. Then we would have to bribe the cop with our day's worth of business and go to bed a bit hungrier than the night before. We rarely saw Mama then, but it didn't matter because we felt like we had become our own people: going to school while making a living, watching out for each other, praying for the good and charging against the bad, never allowing the big, bad mansion to swallow us whole into its darkness—looking at the driveway that Norman had turned into a lot for stolen cars and the main floor he had converted into a copy center for fake deeds.

We were a team, Paolo and I and the van, and we'd found our Common Enemy, the one Papa had warned us about a long time ago. Its name was Hunger, its accomplice Defeat. And we did everything rather than fall prey to Norman, its Commander. But just as in any other war, the good soldier needed to get struck down, get back up, get struck down again, and crawl and fight and even cry his way to glory. But, oh, how I prayed for glory to come sooner.

Paolo and I cried out together. He hid me under his arm, and used his other hand to scramble for a weapon—a bat, a ruler, a brush. Norman had been drinking all day, upset about misprinted deeds and a large bribe to the sheriff, and set his mind on taking out his rage on Mama. When he was mad, he clubbed Mama with a shoe tree and chased her around until they both fell from drunkenness or trauma. Once they passed out, I ran to Mama and found her bruises, rubbing and soothing them while checking for her pulse. Paolo considered kicking Norman in the groin, but backed down, and ran out to the car lot instead. Norman stayed asleep and heavy on the floor, long enough for Paolo to key the Land Cruiser and run to the nearby sari-sari for an ice pack and Band-Aids. That night Mama slept in Paolo's room, crying and groaning in pain. She cried for us, too.

"I'm sorry," she said, half-conscious in our bed. "So sorry."

We showed her our stash of savings and told her about our secret— our van operation and the cool things we did in it. She said she didn't understand, but that she was proud of us, that she had raised such book-smart, street-smart children—the perfect combination of her and Papa.

We enjoyed talking to her, telling her a bedtime story about our life. I showed her drawings I'd made of the van and of our friends, and Paolo played her some songs that were popular on our route. I rolled out a map I'd made of our daily itinerary, which she studied and traced with her red-lacquered finger. Paolo listed the names we'd given each other, emphasizing in the end that a boy five years my senior had called me Prinsesa.

"I think we found her first crush," he said, elbowing me.

"Stop, Kuya!" I said, slapping his elbow.

We jeered and heckled, while Mama held my map up to her face.

"What do you think of our route, Mama?" I said.

"Puñeta. It's brilliant."

"Wake up, sloths," Norman said as he pulled the blanket off us.

"What do you want?" Paolo said, pulling the blanket back on and sitting up as if to shield me.

"Oh, you idiot," Norman said with a grin. "You try to fight me, I fight you back harder. You're gonna pay me back for those wheel mags, sir. Oh, yessir, yessir."

"What do you mean?" Paolo said.

"Get up and get ready—you're going to school early. I got a van service to run," Norman said as he walked away, tossing Paolo's keys from hand to hand. "No one can stop me, you bastards. I own this mansion now and I own you."

Norman took over our business that morning, hiring Tony, one of his cronies, to drive us to school, then to operate our established routes. They made more money than we did because they could make trips while we were in class. His man took a fourth of the profits, while Norman and Mama split the remainder.

Mama fed us with her portion, but our regular meals didn't suffice. Our adventures on the van had grown in us a different kind of hunger—for freedom and friendship. They may have filled our stomachs, but they, too, killed something special in us. They birthed in Paolo a certain kind of sadness, and in me a certain kind of pain.

The following week, Paolo and I each entered our versions of the dark world, me in my imaginative little head, and he at the bar and billiard hall. When together, we continued to listen to the same music upstairs, bobbing our heads in rhythm. Paolo drummed the beat with his finger and cigarette, and forced the words to each song through clenched teeth. I succumbed to my inner world and wrote in my journal: "It can't be a joyride without a few bumps. No, it wouldn't be a joyride at all."

Fowl

1996

I was born too small to have needles puncturing my translucent skin. Mama decided against vaccines, appalled by the thought of seeing her already-unpretty baby lanced in her fatless thighs.

The summer I turned ten, and Tachio would have turned seven, fluid-filled blisters coated my body. Mama quarantined me in my bedroom and said, "You can handle chicken pox. Take this every four hours." She placed a bottle of acetaminophen on the dresser.

"Mama, will you stay and sing to me? Please?"

She began to hum, stroked my hair with her bony fingers, smirked, then stopped, and said, "I can't." She pulled the door behind her and did not return that night nor any night thereafter. I listened to the *click-clack* of her heels as she walked away.

Paolo didn't want to get sick. He was busy with orders. He knocked on my door and spoke from the other side, his mouth pressing against the door frame, and said, "I have deliveries to make. I'll bring home something for you, 'kay? Gum or maybe Choc-nut?"

Malaise would not let me respond.

"It's just to the billiard hall, then back. You know I can't get sick, right?" he said.

Only Manang Biday had intention or permission to come near me. We all somehow believed that her visits to the garbage hill immunized her from air- and waterborne diseases. Her gravelly voice, thick-soled feet, and leathery skin caused us to think that whatever lived under her blackness and inside her Indio-ness was impervious to malady.

She came to my room, rested two tin bowls on my dresser, and rolled me off my sweated-through sheets. The blisters had broken and leaked, and had left imprints of ooze on the bedding. I *ughhh*ed to her touch. She heaved me up from lying down to sitting against the base-board, and fed me Knorr bouillon broth with a spoon. Her arthritic hand shook as she brought the spoon from bowl to mouth. I peeled dry lip from dry lip, dry tongue from the roof of my mouth, as I anticipated the taste of salt. After the last sip, I slid back under my sheets as my eye-lids fluttered. Manang Biday rolled up my sleeves, dipped a washcloth in a bowl of brown vinegar and cooled black tea, and patted the sores on my arms. She rolled me to my side again and patted the sores on my back. She cooled the blisters by blowing onto them. I asked her what they looked like, and she said, "Like chicken skin."

Manang Biday came thrice a day for the next ten days.

"I get sad and bored lying here," I said to her as she attended to my sores.

"Oh, no use complaining now. You need rest," she said. "Besides, you'll have nothing to do out there. Elma's away at the farm now to help my brother."

"Do you not miss her? I miss her," I said. "And does she not get tired of going here and there, to wherever she's needed?"

"That's life for us. We're used to it," she said, wiping sweat off my forehead. "Bahala na ang Diyos." It's up to God.

"Bahala na."

"Next time you step out of your room, you will not recognize this house," she said.

"How so?"

"Chickens."

"The others have chicken pox, too?" I said with pep, relieved that I wasn't the only one stricken.

"No. Real chickens," she said.

I did not recognize our house the morning I emerged from quarantine. The sounds alone made me feel like I had woken up in a busy part of Manila: the city's periphery where, as I'd seen on the news, children swam in the imburnal, pickpockets whizzed through crowds, and people still died of tetanus and malaria.

The sounds and smells struck me. Crowing, squawking, haggling, and a din rose from the floor below. The fetor of sulfur and ammonia entered my nostrils and went straight to my mouth. I retched. The stench was the kind of stench that made you think of colors: dirt brown, fish gray, liver red, and muriatic acid orange.

But because I'd been confined for nearly two weeks, I refused to stay upstairs. I had to investigate. I had to know what had replaced the smell of orchid, jasmine, and ylang-ylang, of orange juice and orange tea, of my mother's freshly laundered robe. I had to know what had superseded my mother's humming, my father's singing, and Katring's and Loring's laughs.

A few years back, the clinking of champagne glasses and the swishing of debutantes' gowns resounded through the ballroom and disco room. That day, babbling boomed through the hallways and arched entryways. I made my way to the main floor where, for every ten scraggy, dark-skinned men, there stood a potbellied male in a short-sleeved linen polo barong, or gusot mayaman. Wrinkles of the rich. Cigarette smoke rose from wherever the men stood. And they stood in circles, as if to gather around a subject worth speculating. I came closer, coughing, breaking through clouds of puffed-out fumes and budging my way through the horde. I snuck between two smokers and saw what was causing a commotion: a chicken.

The rooster sat with its breast and fluff in the cup of a man's hand; his fingers forked between the bird's thighs. The rooster wore all shades of red: a vermilion comb, a ruby-red hackle, a crimson wattle, and a maroon tail. It had a short but sharp beak, blood-black plumage in the torso and neck, and spurs dressed with blades. The handler stroked it from head to tail, repeatedly, as if stroking were part of the animal's breathing. His hands and the bird's feathers were equally oily, making it hard to tell how the grease transferred—from bird to man, or man to bird.

"Hoy!"

Someone grabbed my forearm and towed me to the main steps.

"Aren't you supposed to be in your room?" Tony, Norman's right hand, said.

"I'm better," I said. "I want to see what's going on. It's my house." I shrugged his hand off my still-itchy arm.

"Always so curious," he said, shaking his head. "You want a show? Come with me."

I followed him down the steps to the shaded drop-off, and down the driveway toward the car lot. Plops of moss green and grayish white spread over the ramp connecting driveway and lot. The latter—the floor of which was now also a mantle of ammonia-smelling feces—stored what looked like miniature batting cages. The maids' break room, where Judith and my yaya used to share a Coke while watching a teleserye, now housed stacks of cardboard crates. And from inside the crates, roosters crowed. I knit my brows together and scratched my head.

I knew what was happening. Even though my parents hadn't participated, it was a big enough sport in the country: sabong, or cockfighting, the country's favorite blood sport. Norman and Tony had transformed the downstairs part of the mansion into a breeding and training center, and the main floor into a reception for gamblers. They had set up a gaffing station in one corner of the break room: a tool bench with knives and spurs of varied contours and lengths. On the other end of the room, they had placed a crib mattress on an upturned box, a hospital bed for an injured bird.

"The mansion's prinsesa," Tony said, his hand on my shoulder.

The smoker squatting next to the hospital bed and the gaffer shining a blade walked over to us. They smiled but didn't speak, and went back to their stations. Tony struck a match and lit a cigarette.

"Watch," he said. He reached into a cardboard crate and pulled out a white-and-yellow game fowl. It had an ombré plumage: dandelion at the neck, custard down its spine, and sunbeam and gold through the wings and tail. Tony sucked on his cigarette and puffed a one-two-three onto the bird's face. The bird fanned its tail, stretched its neck, and lifted its white-and-gold wings. Tony puffed again, building a crown of smoke around the creature's head. He let go of it, and it flew one meter off the ground. Pakpak, the Tagolog word for "wing," and the sound the bird made when flapping and showing off its fair-haired feathers. It cracked the atmosphere with its bladelike wings and whipped air from under them. Pakpak. Pakpak. Its right wing flapped a half beat faster than the other, forcing the animal to swerve rather than glide. I shielded my face with my scabby arm, afraid that it would slash or scratch or peck.

"Hinay," Tony said, commanding the bird to calm down. He clicked his tongue, and his fowl friend perched on his forearm. "We call this one Crazy Wing."

Someone applauded.

"You talkin' about the bird or you talkin' about her mother?" Norman said, approaching. "Crazy Wing is one of my favorites. My other favorite still needs a name."

I glowered at him.

"You know what, that red-and-black one upstairs is just like you," he said, pointing his index and middle fingers at me. He licked his lips. "We should name that one after you, Strong Will."

Tony smirked.

Norman formed his hands into brackets and raised them above his head, to hold up his invisible marquee. He said, "It's perfect. Crazy Wing versus Strong Will, our opening show. My moneymaker. Ah, for every win, money for my goons and guns." He wheeze-laughed as he walked away.

"Did he say guns?" I said to Tony.

"Can't say much just yet, but that man and your mother have big political dreams, Prinsesa."

"What dreams?"

"Like he said, goons and guns. Up north. He, the king. Your mom, the queen. And you, some kind of princess."

"Up north, where Mama's from?"

"No, farther north. Where *he's* from. It's bad where your mom grew up, but it's bloodier where he's from. Anyway, showtime soon," he said, puffing smoke onto the bird again. "Back lot." He tapped his cigarette, took one last drag, and stubbed it out on the ground. He kissed Crazy Wing's cape and handed him over to the gaffer, who then wound a leatherlike tape around the bird's leg to attach a blade.

I cringed at the knife edge as it glinted in the sun. I thought of where it could strike and how it could start a bloodbath. Tony took the bird and hugged it into his chest, shading it from the bright sun with his hunch.

"Can't let the fowl see too much sun before a fight. It blinds them," he said, walking to the back lot as I trailed behind.

There was the noise again: crowing, squawking, haggling, and dins. We'd had crowds in the mansion before, but only now did the noise deafen me. Five steps up the cinder-block stairs, and Tony and I were surrounded by a flock of men with sombreros, mustaches, and cigarettes. No breeze disturbed us. And no leaves trembled. The bougainvillea tree bowing over from the other side of the stone wall provided shade, but the air was rank and did not shift.

The men called out numbers and gave hand signals to one another: peace fingers, T for time-out, high fives, all ten, one up, two down, a circle, a fist, and fist against fist. They stood on furniture taken from the lanai and the maids' break room. Beams of light shone on them—not from a chandelier or bulb, but from holes in the corrugated tin roof. A man with outstretched arms, whom they called a "kristo," collected bets as he coasted through the thirty or so bodies.

I fit my way into the middle of the circle, where two parallel chalk lines made a fighting ring. On the inside perimeter of the circle, the potbellies in gusot mayaman sat on wooden benches—which I assumed were the best seats in the house. I continued to inspect Mansion Royale: A Cockfighting Arena.

My eyes moved around the circle and stopped when I spotted my mother.

She wore the same ball gown she had on the night of my third birthday. It fit tighter around her bust and arms, but billowed over her belly. I looked down at my outfit: Paolo's beat-up undershirt that was blotched from my blisters. I crossed my arms in front of me to hide the mess that I was. I looked up at Mama again. She had twirled her hair into a high bun and had painted her lips and cheeks red. Papa would have loved seeing her: pretty, stylish, confident, ready to party, and ready to greet a group of investors. She was Mama from before I turned three, before she slashed the air with a knife, and before she disappeared in the night.

Mama shook hands with those in gusot mayaman. They gave besos while they complimented her looks. She waved a pageant-queen wave, reminding me of Little Benny from the stories she used to tell. *Estrella, the center of her father's campaign speeches and motorcades. Little Benny bonita.*

She caught me glancing at her, or I caught her glancing at me. Either way, I refused to recognize her presence, and she gave the impression of not knowing who I was. She looked past me—waving, making her hair bounce as she moved, and smiling that smile she used for the press.

There.

That's who we had become: living in the same house, but in different worlds. Since she betrayed Paolo and me, and stole our jeepney service, I felt as if I couldn't trust her. And since the night she pulled the door behind her as I moaned through a fever and broke out in sores, I knew that Orchid Mama had either departed the mansion or had died along with my baby brother.

As I watched her, hot air pushed from my abdomen and up to my neck and ears.

The kristo called to the crowd. "Huling taya!" he said. Last bet!

A smoker raised his hand and the kristo whistled. The haggling stopped. The crowd quieted. The trainers entered the ring with birds clutched in their arms. One human-and-animal pair stood to the right of the parallel lines, and the other to the left. A referee—one of Norman's men—indicated that the men should squat. They followed.

Norman stepped into the ring. He announced, "Now as some of you may know, I grew up in Abra. Very poor. We had to make do. We didn't have television, no radio, no cinemas, yeah? But we had chickens. God-fuckin'-fighting chickens, hey!"

Someone in the crowd hollered, "Yeah!"

Norman continued. "My queen and I welcome you to the first cockfight at Mansion Royale!" He gestured with his hand for Mama to step forward.

She took two steps toward the center of the ring and waved. She waved with squinty eyes, looking past people, as if into a fog.

"Make those bets big! The big winner receives a special prize. Let's just say the prize's name is Sampaguita," Norman said.

Strange, I thought, *that they would reward a sabong winner with a tropical flower.*

Norman held up his invisible marquee again, and said, before sitting back down, "Crazy Wing versus Strong Will! Let's begin!"

The trainers stroked the birds, and the birds looked at each other with dimmed, bloodshot eyes. The sportsmen let their gallant birds touch the dirt with their claws, but kept their hands around the birds' breasts. The men lit cigarettes and, as Tony had shown me earlier, puffed onto the game fowls' heads—the smoke as their battle trim.

Then they let go of the cocks. Dust clouds formed around claws, lifting off the ground as the fight commenced. With elongated necks, expanded wings, raised tails, and dancers' feet, the cocks circled each other, pounced, circled each other, and pounced again. They beat their wings and stirred the previously still air. They raised their plumage around their necks: umbrellas to catch drips of blood. They spiked at each other with their talons.

"Yellow! Yellow!" Mama shouted.

And I said, "Red! Red!"

"Sige! Magpatayan kayo, boys!" Norman said. Go! Kill each other, boys!

Crazy Wing flapped, swerved, and poked Strong Will's tail, thigh, and wing with his glinting blade, not letting a millisecond go by without injuring his opponent. Crazy Wing played quickly but clumsily, keen on wounding but inefficient in his attacks. Strong Will took the blows, silently, never cawing, and moved with ease. As the yellow one busied himself with *strrrung!* and *shhung!* Strong Will soared, hovered for a second, and landed with feet firm to the ground, waiting for his enemy to tire out. The patient one leapt up and landed on the other, striking at the neck with his gaff. Both birds were blood black now; it was impossible to tell them apart. But alas, one sank into itself and tipped over. The crowd cheered. Norman applauded. Mama turned away, turned back around, and clapped.

And I vomited.

Tony lowered his head and picked up his dead bird.

Norman held Strong Will overhead for spectators to see, then collected his earnings from the kristo. Gamblers in ripped jeans and sombreros exited through the back gate, while the men in gusot mayaman funneled out of the space in single file down the cinder-block steps and toward the mansion's main floor. Norman and Mama led them to the breakfast room as they all bragged about their winnings.

I followed and crouched behind a jade urn. I saw women in lacy, polyester halter tops and wedged heels welcome the winning group.

"Gentlemen, meet Sampaguita, Gumamela, and Diyosa," Norman said.

The winners escorted the ladies to the ballroom, disco room, and extra bedrooms, kissing their necks and caressing their breasts.

I cupped my hand over my mouth and crouched even smaller to not be seen. But the scabs on my back, legs, and arms kept itching. I think-talked to myself, *Strong Will. You have a strong will.* I trapped my hands in my armpits to keep them from reaching for the scabs and scratching. I told my body to be still—so still that crooks who had taken over my father's house and the ghost who had taken over my mother's body would forget that I was there. I bit my lower lip and whispered to myself, "Remain unseen or they take you to the ring."

Creatures, Great and Small

1997

Paolo was gone. Gone to the mall or the billiard hall or a friend's house for a smoke. Gone with bloodshot eyes and a mind that had holed up in his consciousness or some rift in time. But even then, he was kind and generous to me—sacrificing his meals so I could have a second serving, stealing KitKats or M&M's from the candy store to bring home as a surprise. We still did most things together when he was home—eating the same scraped-out-of-a-can meal, listening to the same music, staying up late and talking about our dreams. But I was turning into a young lady, and he into a phantom.

With every conversation, the pep in his voice got a little bit lower, and the clarity of his words got hazier. He started using fewer phrases and more letters: E, LSD, AC/DC, MJ, and Notorious B.I.G., whom, Paolo kept repeating, had died last March in a shooting tied to the then-prominent East Coast–West Coast rap feud. He repeated that story over and over, inflating and deflating details each time. He obsessed over Biggie's and Tupac's mysterious deaths, and claimed that he could solve them.

"It's just common sense, man. This guy hired that guy to kill the other guy because he was overstepping. He was in goddamn LA when it was clear that Brooklyn was his fuckin' territory. Common sense, man. They killed each other. They fuckin' killed each other."

He stopped talking to me in sentences and instead replaced them with Biggie's chorus about making more money and having more problems, and Tupac's song about the war on poverty, the war on drugs, and the war between cops and bodies.

The swings between his crazed, raving mood and a mopey-dopey state came quickly and frequently.

"Kuya, are you okay?" I asked.

"Yeah, yeah," Paolo replied, head down, eyes half-shut, mouth barely opening. "Just trippin', sis. Just livin', just trippin', just . . . just tryin', sis. You be good, sis. Don't do what I do. You be good because you *are* good, sis."

He reached behind the TV and pulled out a ziplock bag of pills.

"You don't touch this, okay? This is only for hopeless, broken-ass boys like me. Boys who got nothing. You—you have plenty. It's good for me, but it's bad for you."

"Okay," I said and bit my lip to not cry.

I wanted to be good because that's what he said I was and should be. And with that, he put our friendship at stake. To be good, I had to stay away and stay awake. I had to find other company.

Manong Bidoy, Elma's dad, brought home a puppy from the dump. He was disposing of our trash when he found a three-legged brown pooch at the foot of the garbage hill. It was young enough to vaccinate, he thought, so he brought it home, assured that the three-pound mongrel could be made rabies-free. In the Philippines, whatever could be purchased legally was available half off from a bystander or wet-and-dry-goods market, vaccinations included. In exchange for old chafing dishes and utensils from the now-defunct Mansion Royale: A Grand Palace, the stray got an injection and handwritten records. He was officially safe and officially mine.

At first, Manong Bidoy and I were afraid that Mama would disapprove of having such a deformed, disabled creature at the mansion. But after surveying the crooks that had been entering and exiting what had become a turnstile—the main doors—we decided that the little pup was no more appalling nor less sensible than the half-sober, half-naked, half-lying crooks Norman had befriended through cockfighting: beer-bellied forty-something-year-old men and their "for hire" women parading through the house. Mama was out with Norman all day, anyway, scrambling for money by any means. She barely noticed the changes my body was going through, so she wouldn't have noticed that a dog was living at home.

The limping pooch was brown like cocoa, so I named him Milo, after my favorite chocolate drink. He was a true puppy—always following me around, whimpering for my attention, licking my face and hands and ears. He liked to sleep next to the bed, instead of on it, because, I assumed, it was much like sleeping at the foot of the garbage hill. He jumped in the shower with me every morning and sneezed in excitement each time the water hit him. Milo and I were both small-framed and dark and skinny from the shortage of food at home. He had big teeth, an overbite, and a little round pug-like nose. Like brother, like sister. He replaced the brother I lost to infant mortality and the brother I lost to drugs.

With him I played the two games I knew best: house and war. I pushed him around in Tiffany's buggy, wrapped in the swaddle I used to pretend was Tachio. He wouldn't lie still, and instead propped his paws on the front side of the basket, his tongue sticking out to the side, and whimpering.

"Shhh, go to sleep now, baby Milo," I whispered, fixing the end of the swaddle that had come undone.

He shimmied out of the cloth and licked my face.

"Thank you," I said, picking him up from the pram and holding him over one shoulder like a baby. "I don't think you want to play house. Let's try war."

I staggered Paolo's superhero plastic cups in a zigzag on the herringbone-patterned floor. At one end of the obstacle course, I scattered
crumbs of that morning's pan de sal.

"Okay, Milo, you're my army dog now. I'm Alpha, you're Beta, and
this is how we get back to our camp." I slalomed down the winding
track and he followed. "That's it, boy!"

We did several rounds of zipping back and forth, and at the sixth or
seventh turn, I added a challenge. I noticed the day Manong Bidoy brought
the mongrel home that it had a limp but could jump high, up to about
hip height. So I tried a command on him. I yelped "Bravo!" for jump and
another army alphabet letter for down. "Bravo!" Jump. "Charlie!" Down.

He sprang nonstop until we reached X-ray, Yankee, and Zulu.

With a few bread crumbs left on the breakfast tray, I taught my
new best friend how to fetch. I'd heard Papa talk about recovering his
men from the Gulf War, and so I assumed that retrieval was a skill all
soldiers had to have. I threw a plush toy down the corridor, and Milo
instinctively knew what to do. He whooshed to where the toy landed
and returned it to me, his tongue still sticking out to the side, pushing
past his big teeth. Upon retrieval of the toy, he knew to expect a reward:
a pat or a rub and a bit of bread.

When I ran out of pan de sal crumbs, I transitioned us to a game
I used to play with Paolo: building pillow forts. I dragged pillows from
every upstairs room to the corridor, Milo helping to carry the weight of
them with his crooked teeth. He walked backward, his tail and bottom
wagging as he stepped, and his mouth clipped to a corner of a down or
a throw pillow. I piled the rectangles of cushions and feathers the way
Paolo used to instruct me to. Exhausted from playing, Milo climbed
onto our fort and found a crevice between layers of cotton. He circled
and scratched, and slept there, his rib cage and belly rising and falling
with his dead-rat puppy breath. I took the swaddle from the buggy, lay
head-to-head with him, and covered us both with my baby brother's
blanket.

The next morning, still cuddled together on our fort, Milo and I awoke to the banging of tins and the swishing of nets and cloths. Manang Biday weaved through my obstacle course, chasing after a gray-brown-and-white stray cat. Maximo ran parallel to them, swinging a family-size biscuit tin to scoop up the prey. They pogoed right and left, trying to keep up with the fast feline, looking like they were performing a tinikling. Leap, leap, pounce. Leap, leap, pounce.

"Ayay! You two, don't just sit there! Help us!" Manang Biday said, her eyes still fixed on the kitty.

I sprang to my feet and loped to Paolo's bedroom to look for his air gun. Despite the comicalness of the commotion, I knew I had to contribute. It was no joke. At least that's what I then understood from my yaya's and Elma's stories and from Philippine folklore we read at school: cats were bad luck. I found Paolo on his bed, half-asleep, and the air gun on his dresser.

"Where are the pellets?" I asked him.

"What for?" he said.

"A cat strayed into the mansion."

He roused himself so quickly, I nearly thought he had gone back to his old self. "Here." He tossed the bottle of yellow-green BBs. "Get that cat. Last thing we need is more bad luck." He fell back on his bed and snoozed.

School was out for the summer, Elma was away, and my brother played dead on his bed, so I made cat sniping my new hobby. From the trundle drawer I dug out the gun belt I had made years ago and wore it around my hip to hold my gun. I made a map of the mansion and stationed Paolo's plastic army men on parts where I'd seen the unwanted mammal. Milo tracked our prey, and I shot at it from the ballroom or upstairs terrace. The stray sped out of the way faster than the little neon plastic spheres. Frustrated, I sought my big brother's help.

"Kuya, the cat's our Common Enemy," I said. "Wanna trap it with me?"

"What?" he said, lying on the bed and tracing the edge of a vinyl record.

"The Common Enemy, remember? Papa told us we had to team up and beat the Common Enemy."

"Pfft." He covered his face with the record. "We got bigger problems than that cat."

"C'mon, just help."

"I probably should, but I won't. Gotta hide here before they try to get rid of me, too." He started laughing silently again.

"Fine, don't." I shook my head and sighed. I adjusted my gun belt, clicked my tongue to bid Milo to follow, and slammed the door behind me. The pup and I walked downstairs, where I thought we might find sensible, sober company. We found Manong Bidoy and Maximo unreeling a damaged net. I watched them thread an old clothesline through the net's holes, making a giant drawstring sack.

Maximo placed a fish bone on a plastic plate, held it out in front of him with one hand, and pointed at his chest with the other, and said, "Wee-nerr. Me." Winner.

I giggled and gave him a thumbs-up.

Manong Bidoy told me to observe from the ballroom terrace as he gathered his weapons. I ran up with Milo and watched father and son try to take the cat hostage. They spread the net on the ground and propped a rubber tire in the center, inside which they placed the plastic plate. They lured the animal with the bait, waited for it to crouch inside the tire, and seized it by pulling on the clothesline and drawing it closed.

I applauded them from the terrace as Maximo leapt in excitement.

"Wee-nerr! Wee-nerr! Me!" he said, proud of his catch—the pest, the vexation.

I boogied on the terrace along with his cheer. Milo sprang and spun. I chopped the air with karate hands, and said, "Take that, Common Enemy!"

Paolo still vegetated under his sheets, while Milo and I awoke energized from the previous day's feat. Eager for another mission, I decided to change into my day clothes before breakfast. I opened the creaky closet door, paused, and then slammed it on what had just stunned me. I screamed. Milo barked intermittently with my squeals, jumping as I jumped in terror. A few minutes later, help arrived. Manang Biday and Manong Bidoy hastened from downstairs to upstairs with washboard, machete, and net in hand.

"What happened?" Manang Biday said, as she pulled me away from the closet and into the safety of her batik wrap.

I pointed at my closet and said, "In there."

Manong Bidoy motioned for me to keep quiet and tiptoed over. He cracked open the door and found, not a burglar or a rapist or even a roach, but a mama cat licking and nursing three kittens—one white, one brown, and one yellow furry oblong lying in my now gooey, bloody clothes.

The cat had come back to the mansion, not simply to annoy or vex us, but to find a place to labor and birth. It found a dark, cozy private place to have its litter. All the hours I spent outside searching and pursuing our kill, the pregnant cat spent building its nest in my very own room. I felt stupid. And yet, I also felt a fondness for the creatures. How could I not be smitten by three snuggling kittens?

Manong Bidoy hovered his net over the newborns.

"No, don't!" I said, pulling the net before it trapped the purring family. "I'll keep them."

"Bad luck, Neng," Manang Biday said, grimacing.

"But look at them. Even Milo likes them."

Milo had joined the cats. He licked the tops of their heads and sniffed their bottoms.

"What do we do?" Manong Bidoy said.

I walked over to my chest of drawers, pulled out Tachio's old swaddle, and said, "They can live here with me, in my closet. Paolo was right—we have a bigger problem than these cats."

"Bahala ka," Manang Biday said, hands up in the air. Suit yourself and do what you will. She raised her prayer hands up to the sky and said, "I wash my hands clean of this."

"Before you go, can you do me a favor? Can you bring some food for the mama cat?"

"Ayay!" she said, scratching her head. "Fine. But let's hope that birthmark of yours is strong enough to cancel this curse."

I held up my left hand, folded in my thumb, rubbed it over my birthmark, and smiled. "Palad." Palm, and also, luck.

I let the tabbies and toms cradle and grow in my cubby of clothes, and I fed them condensed milk from Manang Biday's kitchen. I told them stories. I read them books and entertained them with Milo's and my tricks. "Bravo! Charlie! Bravo! Delta!"

I swaddled the kittens and pushed them up and down the corridor in Tiffany's buggy as Milo trailed closely behind.

I sang to them, passing on my own lullaby and luck. They were my sunshine now.

I called them mine and grew my own family. Regretful of having shot neon BBs at the mama cat, I gave her a soft chin scratch, rubbed behind her ears, and stroked her from forehead to tail. I named her Lucky.

Halfway through summer, as I revolted at Norman downing a half-dozen donuts for breakfast, Mama surprised me with a brown paper bag that had something chirping inside. I suspected something was at stake.

"A little gift for you from us," she said.

"What for? My birthday isn't until the end of the month," I said, glancing at the brown bag resting next to my plate.

"An early birthday present," she said, then paused. "Since Paolo is no longer living with us."

"What do you mean?" I raised my voice, bringing my hands from my lap to the table. I held my breath.

"He's moving in with his real dad. Not your papa, but my first husband." She explained that the man she had left for Papa had wanted custody of Paolo. And now that he was too much of a burden for her, she had to let him go. She waved her hand in a big swoosh, encouraging me to look around the breakfast room: a muggy space with paint peeling off walls, cracked cornice, spiderwebs, chandelier shades holding dead bugs, and rattan chairs with loose reeds and sticks that had come undone from the weave.

"You can't expect me to take care of this house by myself. I need all the help I can use. Paolo has turned into a vegetable. An *expense*."

Norman interposed. "Rule number one in this house: if you're gonna live here, you better be useful. Look at Elma's family. They get to stay because they contribute."

My lips trembled.

Mama said, decanting the last drop of gin from the flask into her tea, "I can't help him get better, but his real dad can."

"He doesn't even know his dad."

"I said, I can't help him get better."

"Better?! I don't even know what better means anymore!" I snatched the brown bag from the table and huffed and puffed upstairs. I blustered into Paolo's bedroom. "Kuya! Where are you?"

I threw the brown bag onto Paolo's bed and rummaged through his things. I looked in the trundle and behind the TV. His clothes, bags, and vinyl collection were gone. Heat once again balled up in the pit of my stomach, and I wanted to scream it out. But as I was about to let out a cry, the brown bag shook and tipped over. Out popped a yellow chick, its head turning from side to side, one degree at a time, its beak pronouncing something small and sweet.

In exchange for my brother, my mother had gotten me a baby chicken—round and small as my fist. The chick stared at me, its neck

stretched long and its yellow feathers beaming brighter than the tropical sun. It looked happy to see me, eager to know who I was. I knelt
down close to the bed and offered my hand. It hopped on, pecked it,
then chirped.

Not knowing what else to do, I gave it a name. "Hi, Tweetie."

The coquettish tilt of his head, the fluff of the feathers on the back
of his neck, his darling winks and blinks, and curved, dull claws fit not
in the fighting pit, but in a children's board book.

I lay on the bed and it waddled to the crook of my neck. It stayed
there, its fuzz warming my throat and absorbing the tears seeping from
the corner of my eyes.

"Bye, Kuya."

I spent the last days of Philippine summer, the end of May, acquainting
the mammals with the bird. We all slept in my room and shared the tray
of food that Manang Biday brought up from the kitchen. Sometimes
Manang Biday stole chicken feed from the back lot for Tweetie. We
played house and war. When I walked, they followed me like a train
caboose. When I showered, Milo jumped in with me, Lucky licked her
kittens and herself on the bath mat, and Tweetie swam in the sink. The
dog slept next to my bed, the cats in the closet, and the chick on my
chest. They became my motley crew, my family.

The last days of summer also meant that it was the tail end of
cockfighting's peak season. Bird trainers made more than half of their
annual revenue at this time, I heard Tony say. He said that late May and
early June brought thousands of fighters and gamblers into the larger
arenas, temporarily shutting down small-time, back-lot operations like
Norman's. He traveled with Mama and his men to districts such as
Cubao and Muntinlupa, and there fought their best birds. And there

met with mayors, councilmen, and vice-governors, plotting schemes for
the next midterm or term elections.

I came home from the first day of fifth grade, blasting through the
front doors, saying, "Babies, I'm home!"

Milo came limping toward me, frantically barking and biting my
socks.

"What's wrong, buddy?" I said, running upstairs with him.

I opened the door to my room and found the cats cowering in the
closet. Mama cat had her claws and fangs out, and the kittens were bur-
rowed under her. Milo continued barking, jumping and turning, almost
howling and motioning his head toward the door.

"What happened, buddy? Where's Tweetie?"

He barked again, jumped on my leg, and tugged at my school
skirt with his crooked mongrel teeth. Tweetie wasn't in my room nor
my brother's, not in the sink or tub playing rubber ducky, not in my
shoes or slippers. His bowl of chicken feed, which was right outside my
bedroom door, was full and untouched.

I started to cry, knowing that something bad had happened to the
bird I had grown from a yellow chick to a full-breasted, white-feathered
chicken. I ran downstairs to look for Manang Biday, but I didn't find
her. Instead I found, on the kitchen table, roasted poultry—wings,
thighs, full breast, and all.

Norman had lost a bet and his most prized gamecock, and he found
it only fitting to un-celebrate. After a win, he usually roasted a whole
pig to feed himself and his men. But after a loss, or worse, a casualty, he
took away something that was precious to Paolo, Mama, or me.

Norman stood against the kitchen sink. He sweated in his safari
shirt, contorting his Elvis face to a Joker sneer, and petted his second-
best brown-and-crimson derby bird. He clicked his tongue and nodded his head toward the roasted chicken on the kitchen table and said,
"Dinner."

Library

The mansion was dark. Always dark. Always ready to devour me. Always sad. Always filled with men and their women, drinking, smelling of whiskey and San Miguel beer and sticky, quick, heavy-groaning, unfaithful sex. Always filled with fighting chickens—aggressive, unlike my dead Tweetie. Chickens roamed everywhere, pooped everywhere, pecked on everything: the ottoman, the rattan peacock chair, the breakfast table, the record player and turntables, the imperial silk curtains, the Oriental rugs. They laid waste the relics of my parents' empire.

We hadn't had power in the mansion since after my pet chicken was butchered and broiled. I'd learned to line my room with leftover crescents of mosquito coil—ones I'd collected from other rooms after they'd been used as a brothel—to ward off bugs and the obscurity of night. The perimeter of the room flickered like a landing strip awaiting a rescue plane.

SOS.

Save our souls! Save my pets! Save me!

My prayers to God. My tear-drenched, heart-wrenched prayers to the God of the nuns at the convent next door, the God of Elma's family's charismatic church, the God Paolo and I petitioned to when we were lonely and hungry, the God we sang to at the all-girls school, the God that Papa said blessed the crippled, the meek, and the lowly, the God my country had called out to for hundreds of years. Help for them must mean help for me, I believed. And every night I cried that that God would in turn believe I was in need. *SOS. SOS. SOS. Please, please, please.*

Good night, coils.

Good night, books.

Good night, bed.

Good night, pets.

Good night, moon.

Good night, Mama and Papa.

Good night, Paolo.

Good night, baby buried in the garden.

Good night, mansion.

Good night, darkness.

Daytime felt less scary than night. Day meant school, and school meant being elsewhere. Day promised friends my age, teachers who gave lessons and enforced routine, a stocked cafeteria, a gymnasium, and a soccer field set for play.

Mama and Norman dropped me off at school before heading out for the day's shenanigans. In the car, they discussed names of politicians and businessmen and land-owning priests, how each one could be made interested in their hypothetical products or projects. They argued about the most important person in their lives—the sheriff.

"Pay again? We just gave that asshole three thousand pesos, that son of a bitch," Norman said, slamming his hand against the car door.

"Sweetheart, I'm sorry. It's not my fault," Mama said, half-sultry and half-nervous. "We have to pay or he'll padlock the mansion."

"Right." Then he'd reach for Mama's thighs, then between them, then grab.

It made me squirm in my seat.

Mama pulled a rolled-up stack of paper from her purse. "Which one should we sell today?" she said.

Norman took the documents from her hands, shuffled through them, and said, "This one."

Sitting in the cargo space, I leaned in and spied from the corner of my eye. The paper read, "TITLE DEED: This is to certify that Estrella Alarcon is registered as the absolute proprietor of the land and edifice at Palos Verdes."

I remembered the name: Palos Verdes, the pool club where I fell from a slide and hit my head. I knew that we did not own the property. I broke into a sweat and swallowed my spit.

Mama and Norman laughed. She pulled her hair to one side, took her wad of false deeds, and gave it a kiss. He slapped his knees in excitement, wheezed for breath as he laughed, and said, "Mga uto-uto!" Gullible. Ignoramus.

What a relief it was to stop at the school driveway, open the hatchback door, and hop out to my day away from them. What a relief to not have to watch them flatter each other: incubus and succubus rolling around and lurching, tripping over their miseries.

"Hey, do well at school. It's all we have going for you," Mama said, filing her nails in the passenger seat. "See you after aerobics class."

Mama hadn't had a gym membership since the Gulf War. "Sure. See you."

"Don't fuck up school. You lose your spot there and I'll *really* go nuts."

I smirked. "Right."

School mornings started with a chat in the bathroom or by the lockers. All lies. I told my friends, even the humble and genuine ones who could've given me grace or mercy or money, that all was well and that my pet dog was going to the groomer's and my mama was getting me a pair of Guess jeans and my brother helped me with my homework and I watched last night's episode of *Thank God It's Sabado*. Then once they found me likable and amusing enough, I'd offer to draw them a portrait for ten pesos apiece.

"I can color it with glitter gel and mount it on cardboard," I said. "You can put it up on your desk or give it to your boyfriend or post it on your locker."

What an easy sell. Elma and I spent many years drawing people, practicing our craft, the craft I inherited from Papa: design paired with entrepreneurship. With a pack of glitter gel pens, I sketched on cardboard I'd picked from the recycling bin, faces and dresses—all inspired by the many fashion magazines I'd read with Mama—and laminated them with clear packaging tape. Those private school girls belonging to elite families never questioned my rate. If anything, they called it a bargain. I called it lunch.

I did what Mama and Norman were doing: made deals with those who had money and power. But I felt that what I was doing was honest—no cons, with a real tangible product, no forgery, no envelopes passed under the table, no dead birds, and no false deeds.

"Next summer we'll make it up to Abra, and the rest, as they say, is history. Fuckin', fucked by the Spaniards and Americans, Filipino history," I heard Norman say once. "We snag the gubernatorial seat, and damn, that politics money's gonna taste so good."

Unlike him, I wasn't sucking my classmates dry of their money, binding their hands—or mine—with imaginary handcuffs: my mother's make-believe sales, plus Norman's wiles and political ruses. I was surviving and, as I remembered Paolo had instructed me to do, being good.

The school bell rang at seven thirty and rang again at noon. My morning sales ensured my afternoon meal. And that meal afforded me a place at a cafeteria table, an in on a conversation about crushes and schoolwork and R-rated movies and shaving legs, a place where every preteen girl should be: away from hunger, isolation, and insecurity. Lunch was my place to be a normal kid again.

After lunch were three more hours of class. English and history were the only subjects I hadn't nearly failed. With the distractions at home and the lack of light at night, I could never do my homework. With an empty prelunch stomach, I couldn't concentrate during morning periods. I fared well with my English and history work because they came natural to me: stories. Papa used to tell us stories and made it seem like English was stories about people in other people's heads, and history was stories about people on earth, dead or alive. One was crafted to tell truth, and the other to tell facts. I understood—no studying at home required.

I admired my English and history teachers. In forty-minute blocks, they warped us out of the mansion, out of the classroom, out of Manila, and out of the Pacific. The English teacher, Ms. Ria, read Shakespeare, Milton, Whitman, Poe, and Plath to us. The history teacher, Mr. Santiago, introduced us to José Rizal, a writer and our national hero.

Mr. Santiago sat on the teacher's desk, his legs dangling and swinging over the front side. He picked up a pen and twirled it with his fingers, and said, "What is this?"

The class said together, "A pen."

"This is more than just a pen," he said, smoothing his finger across to the felt tip. "This is a revolution."

While the rest of the class furrowed their brows, pursed their lips, and scoffed at him, I fixated on the pen. Mr. Santiago's way of storytelling reminded me of Papa's. They both turned everyday items—coins, maps, pens—into motifs for fables and epics.

"José Rizal freed our country from Spanish oppressors by writing about the nation's ills," he said, picking up and brandishing a book entitled *Noli Me Tángere. Touch Me Not.* Rizal, born an Ilustrado and educated in Europe like my lolo, wrote books to expose friars and unjust treatment of Filipinos.

"Have you ever heard that phrase 'The pen is mightier than the sword'? It's true."

I uncrossed my arms, leaned forward, and mirrored his facial expression.

He ended the class by saying, "And I think some of you here will one day wield a pen for a good cause, a purpose."

At dismissal, I packed my bag, pushed my chair under the table, and sighed out the anxiety over what to do for the next several hours. Mama forgot to pick me up, always showed up at the school gate as late as 8:00 or 9:00 p.m. Five or six hours to kill, five or six hours to wander on campus, lying to my classmates and teachers as to why my mother had not picked me up. "Late business meeting." Or "The new office is under construction and they probably just ran into some issues. Don't worry, she should be on her way. I'll be fine. I've sent her a message on her pager."

And there the hunt began.

After school, I searched for soda bottles and returned them for the two-peso deposit. A snack cost ten to fifteen Coke, Sprite, or Fanta bottles, and dinner about twenty to thirty a plate, depending on the viand. The best place to find the bottles was at the foot of the steps, where girls late for the next period left half-consumed beverages as they hurried to class. Glass bottles also marked the perimeter of the soccer field and basketball gym. Before me they gleamed and beckoned: one rich girl's trash is a poor girl's dinner.

Of course, I had to be sly about it. I couldn't just barrel through school corridors like a homeless person with a shopping cart of junk. Finesse, my mother taught me, was a secret scrounger's armor. I walked behind the lower- and upper-school buildings, instead of down the main hallways. I took the emergency exits instead of the main doors. I spied for bottles from the bleachers, pretending to watch the cheerleaders and volleyball players practice.

My yellow-checkered skirt had pockets deep enough to hold a bottle, and my backpack—lined with crumpled paper to soundproof against the clinking of glass—held up to ten. Each trip to the cafeteria's back window was twelve bottles: twenty-four pesos, or half a meal. Two hours of work bought me supper and killed nearly half of my lonely waiting time.

At home, glass crystals from the chandelier had been my treasure. At school, glass bottles were my loot.

After my work was done, I had three to four more hours to spend at school. By then, the janitors had cleaned classrooms and were weeding the field or disinfecting bathrooms. The Philippine sun had begun to set, painting the sky purple, then pink, then orange, and then swiftly, as though night longed to take over, blacked-out black. It was then that I hid in the library.

The library promised not only shelves of books but a kind of giant public living room that allowed me to be around people *and* have privacy—the balance I needed for my double life. It provided air-conditioned space with a sofa, armchairs, desk chairs, and beanbags. I didn't feel lonely, but I could also keep to myself. I picked a neglected aisle, the geophysics section, and cried a little and let myself be weak for a minute or two. Then I took a cleansing breath, smiled, made a turn into the magazine section, and la-di-da all over again. A new face.

On clammy late afternoons and shadowy evenings, the library housed an assembly of girls-school outcasts. Kyra Kleptomania, who stole ring pops and cookies from the snack cart. Jaqui the Beanstalk, who towered over the short Southeast Asian student body at five foot eight and moved as though her limbs were made of wet sand. Zandra, whose celebrity mother appeared on TV so frequently and, like Mama, often forgot to pick up her daughter from school. Marissa, who had a mustache and considered pathological lying a sport. I assimilated into peer groups just fine, as long as nobody knew of the shortage at home and of Norman's creatively abusive ways.

A library was the missing part of the mansion: the one room the architect forgot to sketch on the blueprint. Of all the sections of the house—ten bedrooms, three maids' quarters, one gym, one lanai, one breakfast room, one ballroom, one disco, and one bar—not one was considered for keeping books. Odd, because Mama prized education—the one inheritance from her Ilustrado upbringing that poverty could not take away. Had they created a space with built-ins and studies, I would've had a refuge apart from my bedroom at home. But, had there been such a sanctuary, Norman surely would've converted it into something filthy—a chamber for drinking or housing chickens. He would've torn apart the books, pulled out pages, and turned them into a cot for whoring. Or he would've knocked down desks, sawed them in half, and fashioned them into a pen for his fighting cocks.

The library was better off at school.

I spent hours getting acquainted with works by Frances Hodgson Burnett and Scott O'Dell. They spoke to me in the language of my heart: fiction for the young.

The day I flipped open *A Little Princess*, I felt as if I weren't alone. In the story, a bookish girl named Sara Crewe lost her father and befriended a servant named Becky. Sara had once lived in an opulent mansion, but her father's disappearance and the First World War had forced her to live in an old attic and give up her toys and clothes.

When I read *Island of the Blue Dolphins*, I thought I was Karana, the girl left stranded and alone on an island. She, too, had a brother whose curiosity led to trouble. He died after being brutally killed by a pack of feral dogs. Karana hunted, made weapons, and built a home out of whalebones to survive. She loved the water, domesticated animals she encountered, and developed a kinship to them. She had a friend, Tutok, a domestic helper on a ship that docked on the island. Reading *Island*, I imagined Paolo as the curious and lost brother, and Elma as Tutok.

I pictured Milo as the otter and Lucky as the red fox. I reincarnated Tweetie as Lurai, the tame bird. I imagined the mansion as a deserted isle, moored to the seafloor, marooned, inaccessible, isolated, and wild.

Sara believed that she would one day be reunited with her father. Karana boarded a ship and sailed for California. They showed me that it was possible: to leave a once upon a time and enter an ever after.

I checked out a book from the library and brought it home, optimistic after being hesitant for so long. *Why take a book home if there was no power and you had no light to make words visible on a page?* I had started reading a book by J. D. Salinger: *The Catcher in the Rye.* In it a boy kept think-talking about all these "phonies." His name was Holden and he talked, walked, and wore his hunting hat all angry, all pissed with the way adults lived and treated him. He went to an exclusive private school and felt as if he had to get away. Just like me.

Salinger's words sounded too honest and too familiar to put down. Holden's voice and angst transfixed me.

I signed my name on the borrowing card, slid the card back in the pocket on the back of the book, and took Holden home.

That night, as I entered through the mansion doors, I patted around for leftover mosquito coils, folded the hem of my shirt into a pouch, and collected in it bits of pyrethrum repellent. Then I walked up to my bedroom, escorted by Milo and welcomed by the cats, and knelt down by the window. I emptied the contents of my shirt onto the floor and picked up the coils piece by piece, laid each one around me, instead of along the perimeter of the room, and lit them. I unzipped my backpack, took my notebook out, opened it to a blank page, and wrote, in bullet points, names of people—real and imagined—that reminded me of who I was or wanted to become: Mr. Santiago, Rizal, Karana, and Holden. I also made a list of goals, mantras passed down by my brother, father, teachers, and friends.

Be good. The pen is mightier than the sword. Do not trust all grown-ups—they are phonies. Fight the Common Enemy. Do all it takes to survive. You are Prinsesa ng mga Tala. You are made of light.

I tore off the pages and taped them to my mirror, then stepped back into my ring of coils, my halo of half helixes.

A votive circle. A vigil for inner peace.

The coils arranged close together brought an illumination that was small but bright enough to let me read. I pulled *Catcher in the Rye* out of my backpack and recited lines from the page. The book and I enshrined in the center, aglow, like a nun in a chapel holding the Book of Common Prayer.

God was now speaking to me, telling me to keep the faith and promising me an escape. He spoke not through scripture nor through the retelling of parables by a priest, but through angsty, tormented Holden Caulfield, and all the other voices in the books I had read. At the turn of every page I breathed in, felt my heart tighten and release, and said, as the nuns next door repeatedly sang, "Amen."

Amen.

Aqua Vitae

1997

I knew the mansion had been deteriorating more and more. The lack of air-conditioning trapped humidity in and caused mold to spread on walls and floors, and paint to peel off in strips wider than my hand. Every storm tore off terra-cotta shingles and allowed rainwater to leak in. And the shortage of household help or concerned adults left foliage uncontrolled and creeping up our stone walls. The water hyacinth in the pond and paddy had grown to its meter peak. It sprawled and matted over the mere, clogging irrigation, trapping odors, stealing oxygen from the fish, and creating plenty of room for mosquitoes. The birds-of-paradise in the garden had died, and the Indian mango trees were now laden with nonvenomous snakes.

But this, water not running through pipes and coming out of the tap, I hadn't foreseen. Water wouldn't come out of the spout in the upstairs bathrooms.

I thought to inspect the faucets on the main floor. I walked down the steps, down the long dark hallway, past the secret door and through the breakfast room, where Norman sank in Mama's peacock chair, napping, feet up on the table, his shoes caked with mud and chicken turd. I snuck past him and into the bar, where my yaya used to serve me

refreshments and teach me the letters in my name. I walked up to the
bar sink and turned the now-rusty hot and cold faucet handles.

Drip, drip, drip.

The last drips of water in the mansion circled around the faucet's
mouth, cumulated into a bead, and trickled into my palm.

I licked it.

And I licked it again until tears replaced the moisture in my hands.
I cried. I knew that this was not a beginning, but an end.

Norman moseyed into the bar, yawning, stretching, the corners of
his lips frosted with drool. He warbled like Elvis about hound dogs not
being high-class and crying all the time. His muffled trill grew louder
as he approached.

He saw me hunched over the sink and said, "Yep, no more water."
He stopped paying the water bill, he explained, because he was saving
money for a big political project and there was no point paying for a
utility if the government only let us have it for four hours a day.

"Damn El Niño sucking these islands dry of water. It's a fuckin'
archipelago in the middle of the fuckin' Pacific—and no fuckin' water.
You, Miss Upper-Class Kid, better get used to living like the rest of this
goddamn country. No food, no power, and now, no water. You know
how I grew up? This. Just like this. With nothing. My cousins, they all
worked for the governor because there was no other work. They killed
and got killed for the governor. I got out of that place and swore that
I'd only come back if I were *the* governor."

I turned around and stared him down, my eyes burning.

"Whatcha lookin' at me like that for, Strong Will?" he said. "I'm
just makin' conversation, geez. Just makin' you a, how should I put it?
A well-rounded person." He pulled out a chicken foot from his safari
shirt pocket—one that belonged to his deceased fighting bird, the one
he named after me. He stroked the claw and the spur still attached by
a rubber band, and traced the crumples and rumples on the dead bird's
skin. "You're welcome, miss."

He kept talking, expounding, while caressing the severed claw. He explained that just hours ago, he had pawned his wristwatch, sold a couple of his fighting chickens, and gave Milo to the sheriff's son. "Sheriff was gonna padlock the house. I had to pick between the dog and the mansion, Strong Will. And besides, my chickens were frightened of that mongrel."

I sucked in my lips, scrunched my shirt's hem with my fists, flared my nostrils, and shook my head from side to side. I stepped into a wider stance, breathed in, and aimed my forehead at Norman, like a bull about to charge. And right as I was about to lunge, he turned and walked away, and resumed singing about catching rabbits and me not being a friend of his.

He was no friend of mine either.

I swiveled back to face the faucet and breathed through my teeth. I stared at the spout and prayed water into existence, mouthing, "Please."

The school chaplain once said at Wednesday Mass that Jesus walked on water and another time he turned water into wine. I figured that Jesus was well practiced in hydromechanics, and that he wouldn't refuse showing off his holy powers to a thirsty girl like me. That Friday night I learned that Jesus sometimes said yes in ingenious ways.

"Have faith," Papa had said. Jesus was God, after all.

"Neng! Neng!" I heard the call of a friend and the footsteps of an eager playmate.

"Elma! You're back! What are you doing here? Look at you," I said, studying the bends and bows that now outlined her body.

Her uncle's rice farm had no harvest at all. They tried to save the little bit of grain they could, but everything had dried up. They sent her back to Manila because they had no food or water to pay her family with and because Mama said she could use some help—and that I could, too.

"It's not any easier here," I said. "Norman cut off the water. See?" I reached my cupped hand under the tap.

"My mama told me. But at least you and I are together, right?"

The next morning, I woke up to the smell of peanuts.

"You hungry?" Elma said, holding a pan de sal roll over my face, teasing me with the scent of freshly ground peanut butter. "It's your favorite—pan de sal with peanut butter from my mama's mortar and pestle. Mmmmm-mmm-mm."

I reached for my favorite sandwich.

"Not so quick, friend," she said as she snatched the roll away from my hand. "You gotta work for it."

"What do you mean?"

"Today is the day you will learn how to fetch water."

When we reached the back lot—where Manang Biday's family's shack stood amidst the vestiges of Norman's failed fight-and-gamble business—Elma handed me a family-size ice-cream bucket and a gallon gasoline jug. She told me that I could start with two small containers and work my way up to three, maybe four, vessels, if I managed to learn how to balance wooden beams on my shoulders. For a good part of the morning, Elma bossed me around like I used to boss her around, enticing me to work by dangling the highly coveted, cellophane-wrapped peanut butter roll from her belt clip. She said that I could have my breakfast if, and only if, I brought home two full containers of water from the pozo.

"You're taking me to the pozo? Are you crazy?" I said, dropping my jug and bucket on the concrete ground.

"No choice. It's the only way you can have clean water. Do you want drinking and bathing water, or don't you?" Elma said, picking up my containers.

"I do. But you know . . . You know that . . ."

"That only poor folks fetch water from the pozo?" she said. "Look, nobody will even know. We aren't so bad, you know."

"I didn't mean it that way. It's just that I have nothing left." It was true. I had no food, no money, no parents really, and now, no water. I had enough trouble pretending at school. And now I'd have to lie about this, too. I'd have to pretend I'd never fetched water on foot with an old ice-cream bucket and a gasoline jug.

"You have no choice now. I won't always be around to bring you peanut butter rolls or water or whatever, you know?" Elma wanted to go to vocational school and maybe become a secretary, or learn math and open her own sari-sari. Her mama said we all needed to learn to survive while we lived at the forsaken house and that we all needed to find a way out. So I started here, fetching my own water.

"Thank you," I said, reaching back for my bucket and jug. "You've changed, by the way. You're starting to act and look like a grown-up."

"I'm a lady now," Elma said, hands on waist. "While I was away at the rice farm, I got my first period."

"Oh, my!" My eyes widened and my hands pressed on my abdomen. I had forgotten that Elma was a couple of years older than I was.

"It's not too bad. It hurts sometimes, but not too bad. As long as you keep yourself clean, you're good. And soon you'll get yours, too. So that's *another* reason why you need water, diba?"

We walked two and a half kilometers, past the rice paddy and the convent, deeper and deeper into lower-class country. My hands hurt from gripping onto the bucket and jug, and they hadn't even a drop of water in them yet. My flip-flops turned black from the road dust that had collected under my soles. My stomach ached for the roll still cellophaned and tied to Elma's waist. I sweated what I couldn't afford to sweat.

Elma poked me on the side to tickle me while we walked and said that I shouldn't look so desperate, even when I *am* desperate. She said that the cure for anything, even thirst or hunger, was laughter, and that

I should tell her jokes Paolo used to tell me. So we walked some more and told jokes, like two sisters glancing at each other before each punch line, and giggling and swift-stepping, side by side, clutching our vessels like the fishing poles and baby dolls we once had considered our treasure. We were sisters by need, sisters of pursuit, sisters in exploration of teendom and in search of clean water.

After our thirty-minute trek, we arrived at the oasis: a four-by-four cement square with a pole, lever, and spout sticking out of the ground. The pole drew mineral-rich groundwater from forty-five meters below. The lever pumped pressure in and out of the pole, a device that children in line before us rode like a three-hundred-pound seesaw, pushing all their weight down into the simple machine to pull the water up, and kicking off the ground to release the lever and let the water run out of the spout. The pozo was a playground of a special sort, a mix between a water park for the young and a water source for the poor.

I loved it.

At our turn, Elma motioned for me to arrange our buckets and jugs from biggest to smallest—the largest container positioned closest to the spout in case we were hurried out of our spot in line—collecting as much water as we could on the first try. Then she straddled the lever and told me to do the same and cued me to push with a *one, two, three*. Then *mmmmmmph*, we drew the water up. *Uuuuunnnh*, we kicked and drew the water out. Up, down, up, down, sisters on a seesaw, fetching water for the day. Up, down, up, down, hard work combined with the innocence of play. Norman had no idea what I was experiencing, enjoying, learning to do. Mama gallivanted day and night with him, conning people with fake titles and deeds and invisible products, and going by different names: Rosinda, Anita, Carmelle. And there I was— embracing our new level of poverty, caught in the rhythm of play and the momentum of sweaty, low-class Indio work. And the spritz of cool groundwater that splashed off the concrete square and onto our limbs, necks, and faces freshened body and soul, wakened senses from long ago. I understood in that moment of up-down-splish-splash why Jesus was always playing around with water—walking on it, turning it into wine, bathing people in it, washing feet, meeting shamed women at a well.

My dire circumstances taught me to drink deep—to live a life of *life*: crying from the marrow, laughing from the gut, working with every muscle, acting and reacting with ten fingers, ten toes, five senses, and a sixth one . . . the heart.

The water at the well smelled rich, not of chlorine, but minerals, the scent of a waterfall cutting through the stench of the ghetto's *imburnal*—sewage canal. Water from the spout hit the bottom of buckets and jugs with a slosh that warped us out of Metro Manila and into the beaches of Siargao, Boracay, and Palawan, the hem of the Pacific I'd never seen.

"Remember when the mansion was flooded?" I said, sitting on the cool concrete and leaning against the back side of the pozo.

"Good times," Elma said, sitting next to me and spritzing my face with water from her fingers.

"I pushed you in," I said, elbowing her and smirking.

"You almost killed me," she said and elbowed back.

"I taught you how to swim."

"Yeah, well, I taught you other things." She dipped her hand in a bucket and splashed me.

I splashed her back. "Tsunami!"

We snuck our half-empty buckets under the spout and refilled them. "Okay, that's enough wasting water. Except for this one." She splashed me again. "Tidal wave!"

The water hit me right in the head and cooled my scalp. I shook my head like a dog to dry my hair and said, "Isn't it strange that we'd never been in the ocean and yet we know what it's like?"

"Yeah, we know that it's both loud and quiet. I love that it's both of those things."

"How do you think we know so much about it?" I said.

"Movies?"

"Maybe. But maybe it's just one of those things." By *those things* I meant the things that lived in my heart: the things that I had daydreamed about in class, the things that made me reread lines and dog-ear pages of books, the things that made me pause while playing, the things that I'd never encountered and yet could meticulously and exhaustively imagine and sketch.

The coolness of groundwater buried deep and away from the touch of the sun felt like aloe on burnt skin; it kissed and closed my pores. Its taste, however, remained a mystery. I formed my hands into the shape of a bowl and scooped a drink from the bucket. And as I brought my hands to my mouth, Elma slapped my wrist.

She shook her head, saying, "We filter, we boil, and then we drink. Never touch the water with your lips until you've filtered and boiled it, understand? You can die, you hear me? You can die."

After a morning's work and play, Elma and I hit the path back to the mansion. Our feet flip-flopped down the unpaved road, dirt dusting off the ground and sticking to our wet ankles and toes. Elma held her containers with no trouble, with the inner reserve of physical strength that belonged only to an Indio. I, on the other hand, grappled and fumbled and spilled. I braced the ice-cream bucket on my front side with both arms, while the gasoline jug, yellow as the sun above us, hung from my first four fingers with the weight that reminded me just how valuable the contained resource was. The seam of the yellow plastic handle pressed onto my knuckles and, at our fortieth step back to the mansion, skinned the fold of one finger, then two, then another. To save the fourth, I let go of the bucket, spilling half of my morning's work on the El Niño–stricken ground.

"Oh no!" I said. "My water!"

"What did you do? Why did you let go?" Elma said.

"Can we go back? Can we fetch more water? I won't drop it this time, I promise."

"No. It's almost afternoon, and it's Saturday. The line is too long now and no one will let us cut in line on their weekend off." Saturday was water day. Everyone collected water for the week ahead. Sundays are church days, so no one fetched water then.

Saturday.

"I'm sorry, Elma, but I don't think this'll be enough," I said, still bracing my ice-cream bucket.

"You can have some of mine, and you'll just have to skip your bath."

"I can't be dirty!"

"You can't afford to be clean."

"I can't stay at my school if I'm dirty."

"Then do a sponge bath with very little water. Just make do."

"Elma, you don't understand, I have to be clean. It's an exclusive private school."

"Clean the important parts and you'll be fine."

"No, I can't," I said, starting to cry.

A teenage boy, pedaling a tricycle, stopped in front of us. He called us dalagitas, young ladies, or more specifically, *almost* young ladies. "Can I help?"

"Pouty over here spilled half of her water," said Elma.

"Miss Maganda," he said. Beautiful. "I can help you get more water, Miss Maganda."

"Che!" she said, furrowing her brows and blushing from ear to cheek. "I have no time for pedicab boys calling me things."

"Sorry, miss. Just trying to make you smile. You two look like you've had a long morning. Let me help. Please." He patted the duct-taped cushions on the sidecar.

I got in the trike, followed by Elma, who, for the first time all morning, had nothing to say. She looked straight ahead, never glancing at the boy or me. She disregarded my ignorance and his town-boy affection.

"Dalagitas, stay here. I'll take care of it," the boy said as he rallied our empty and half-empty containers.

Neither of us responded nor moved.

A minute later, Elma handed me the pan de sal roll. "Here."

Embarrassed still by my spilling, I took the soggy, sweaty cellophaned sandwich. I unwrapped it, broke it in half, and gave her a piece. She quickly grabbed and munched on it. We said nothing when the boy came back and nothing all the way home. The boy cranked and curbed on his three-wheeler. The swishing of water filled the muggy mosquito-filled air.

"Salamat," Elma and I said in unison as we stepped off the sidecar. The boy saluted us and pedaled away.

"Salamat, Elma," I said.

Elma shrugged and smiled, then picked up her buckets. I walked back to the upstairs bathroom, and Elma to her shack, taking our containers to our designated parts of the mansion.

I decided to store my containers in Paolo's old bathroom. On Sunday morning, I gave myself a sponge bath with five centimeters of water, leaving twenty-five more in the ice-cream bucket and thirty in the jug. I did the math on paper, scheduling my week's ration: fifty-six centimeters in total made about nine centimeters per day. From Sunday morning until Friday night, I would measure the water with Paolo's old ruler, and use a couple centimeters for drinking and five for washing my hands, hair, and body. When I sponge-bathed, shampooed, or washed my hands, I stood in the middle of a basin, collecting the used water for flushing the toilet.

My system worked on the first day, the Holy Sabbath. I rejoiced in my white Sunday dress as though it were my own baptism day. *Fetching water and storing it and using it were rites of some sort,* I thought. From the terrace next to Paolo's old room, I listened to the convent's call to worship. I sat with my legs dangling between the terrace rails, swinging them back and forth to the rhythm of the church bells. I stretched out my hands through the slats, reaching for the voices calling to the Living Water. I praised with the nuns and parishioners, not because I understood who or what or why they were worshiping, but because I knew what it was to have something to drink. To have water and to enjoy it—*that* was my devotion. My song of gratitude for something physical merged with, transformed into, the adoration of the spiritual. The nuns sang and I echoed. Our prayers rose like the smoke of incense, dancing, to the heavens. *As the deer pants for the water brooks, so pants my soul for You, O God.*

Elma and her family spent their day at El Shaddai, the charismatic church that met at the Quirino Grandstand stadium. Mama and Norman woke up at 4:00 a.m. for an early drive to Abra, the province where Norman's mother was from. They had a new venture up in the northern mountains, Mama said. She assured me, by handwritten note slipped under my bedroom door, that the venture—something political—would make us rich again.

I left the note where I found it.

I took advantage of daylight and finished my homework, penning poems and reading about direct and indirect objects by the window. I watched parishioners in their charcoal-pressed ochre, orange, and batik clothes, walking home from church while carrying their babies on their hips, exchanging food wrapped in banana leaves with relatives and neighbors along the way. *So happy and so normal,* I thought.

I kept working to wash away my loneliness. I swept the upstairs floor, polished the handrails, wiped the life-size mirror free of streaks, and changed my sheets to a crunchy set of linens that hadn't been touched since my yaya left. I finished my portrait orders from school—a caricature for Ma-an and a neon name tag for Paola.

Work made me thirsty, and I had a little more than two centimeters of water reserved for the day. I rewarded myself with giant gulps of refreshment, scooping it out of lidless containers with my last Minnie Mouse cup.

At sundown, I ate the plate of rice and sardines that Manang Biday had left for me. Then I brushed my teeth under moonlight with the last of Sunday's reserve. Into bed I went, tucking myself under crunchy covers smelling of mothballs; I spent the night reading by the light of mosquito coils. I fell asleep mouthing words off the page, convincing myself that words made my world a little less lonely. Words were my friends. And water, too.

On Monday morning, I woke up at half past four with a bit of a stomachache—more of a side cramp than a full-belly discomfort. I brushed my teeth, washed my face, and drank my morning helping of water in the dark. Mama and Norman still hadn't come home from Abra, and according to her note, she had prearranged a gypsy cab to take me to school.

I waited for the cab in front of the wrought-iron gates and hopped in as soon as it pulled over. I closed my eyes for a nap in the cab, but my side cramp wouldn't abide. It morphed into a churning in my lower abdomen, a come-and-go twisting sensation in my gut. After the hour-and-a-half ride, I had sweated out my morning's serving of water, creating a ring of dampness around the collar of my checkered uniform.

I stepped out of the cab, dragging my backpack behind me and clutching my stomach. I gasped out invisible O's, then a howl. The twisting in my lower abdomen stretched down to my legs, numbing them so that I could only walk four steps a minute. The school was empty, except for the janitorial staff mopping hallways and watering plants. I padded along, one foot at a time, weakening with every step.

Then something watery leaked out of me: through my underwear, down my leg, and into the ruffle of my sock. It stank. Before I could look down and inspect what had happened, I fell to the floor, faint and unable to motion my limbs, convulsing. A fly landed on my forehead, then another, until five or six or ten swarmed to the rank stench. The first fly bounced on my face as my eyes flickered closed. I slept.

"Papa! Papaaaaa!" I screamed myself awake.

"Shh, shhhh, shhhhh," a lady whispered as she patted my forehead with a damp cloth. "You're having a nightmare. It's okay, you're at the school clinic. The janitress brought you here."

"Oh no. I had . . ."

"I know. I cleaned you up. Okay, ka na. But you're a little feverish and dehydrated, possibly from food poisoning. Do you remember what you last ate?"

"I ate . . . last night. Sardines and rice."

"Did it smell funny, look funny, taste funny?"

"No. I don't think so."

"Anything else?"

"No. Just water. Some last night, some this morning."

"Filtered, boiled, and covered, wasn't it?"

I shook my head.

"Oh, hija." She handed me a glass of water from the stand-up dispenser.

I drank it quickly.

The nurse got up to talk to the doctor. They shook their heads as they murmured to each other, glancing at me at the end of each sentence. I avoided eye contact. They must have found out my secret—the barrenness and filthiness of the mansion. *What girl who goes to this school gets sick from drinking water at home?*

I stayed at the clinic until dismissal time, staring at my feet and the white sheets, which smelled like Clorox. I remembered the afternoon at the pool when the slide flung me to the ground. I missed Paolo and Papa. I missed having a family.

The same gypsy cab that took me to school that morning took me home in the afternoon. Still weak and sad, I moped upstairs with nobody there to ask me, "How was school?" I slouched my way to Paolo's bathroom.

The ice-cream bucket and gasoline jug were still on the corner tile. Every step sent trembles through the ground, rippling the water in the containers. As I got closer, the rippling seemed more like flickering—pricks and pinches breaking through the water's surface.

I screamed as I whacked the bucket and jug over. And I kept screaming—slapping and shaking and kicking the disgust off me.

My week's reserve covered the tile floor—and in it, mosquito larvae wriggled. The micro-tailed babies battled for space in the remaining water, fighting not to slurp down into the drain. I had ingested—sometime between yesterday and that morning—God knows, tens, maybe hundreds, of those larvae.

I ran to the terrace.

"I hate you, Norman!" I screamed, leaning forward against the banister, projecting unto the emptiness before me. "And you, Mama, I hate you, too! You did this to us! To me, to Paolo, to Tachio, to Papa!"

I took a breath.

"Papa, please come get me now! Come back now, Papa. I need you, Papa. Please, get me out."

I sat on the floor, next to the terrace banister, fitting my legs and arms through the slats, and pressing my face between two bars as I looked out at the convent. The nuns made no singing sound and the bells were silent as I sobbed myself dry, the last bit of my energy vanishing.

"Halika na," Elma said as she hoisted me up from behind. Come now. She must've heard me scream. "Tomorrow the nuns will sing again and tonight we fetch more water."

We had legs, we had arms, and we had our prayers and each other. This was not the end. I tried to remember, this was the beginning— fetching my own water.

"There's another life for you and for me," Elma said. "You will get out, I promise."

"I will?" I said, resting my weight on her.

"You will get out of here and find the ocean." She said nothing more as she placed my arm around her neck and limped us off the terrace and down the steps. She hushed me and smiled for me, her crooked mouse teeth peering through. Her crooked teeth reminded me of the day we met, when I locked her in a cabinet under the stairs in Mama's basement closet, in between silk and cotton layers, nearly suffocating her in hopes of keeping her with me at the mansion.

We walked, arm in arm, back to the pozo. Our legs, slender from work and little food, swift-stepped together, once again beckoned by cool groundwater.

Woman at the Well

I had been fetching my ration of water on foot from the pozo for four months now and had grown confident in my abilities. I seldom needed Elma—who had found work and an apprenticeship at the wet market— to accompany me on trips.

I waited until dusk to start my route. I had learned that sunset meant most poor folks were preparing dinner, either for themselves or for their masters. At that time of day, the pozo was mine.

The air at half past five filled with a melodic whispering coming from the well.

The sweet singing called me to my destination, not hastily but with the slow summoning of a mother waiting for her children to come home. I felt my heart as it had been—empty, like the bucket and jug I had brought with me. And there she was, singing, pumping water from the pozo with the strength of her arms and the grounding of her legs. Singing, soothing, with a voice coming from a soft, supple bosom.

Her hair, gathered on one side as she pumped water, fell to her waist, wisps long and black as a moonless night. But no, there was a moon—her face crowning her five-foot-seven body. She kept singing.

She bent down to sit on an overturned bucket and proceeded to wash her hair. She sang some more.

Enamored, enraptured, I inched closer, a deer panting for water. I drank in her voice, my lips parting to taste the sweetness that tropical flowers gave off at eventide. A moonflower, yes, that's what she was: mestiza, tall, vining to celestial skies, and blooming after hours. Evening's blue light made her glow.

"Hello," she said, interrupting her song.

"Hi."

"I'm Diyosa."

"A goddess?"

"Something like it," she said, tousling the tips of her hair.

"Do you live here? I've never seen you here before."

"I live in your house, actually. At least for the time being," she said, rubbing the roundness of her belly hidden behind her perfect hair.

"My house? The mansion?"

"Yes. I've come through many times, late at night, likely when you were sleeping."

"At night?"

"Let's just say I used to work there, and now I live there. It's complicated to explain to a young girl like you. But now that we live together, we can be friends."

Before I could respond, she continued her singing.

I knew, when I saw the cantaloupe-sized roundness of her belly, that she was one of the lady workers, what one of Norman's men called "joy givers," who came through the main doors late at night, when Norman turned the mansion into somewhat of a post-cockfight no-tell motel and rented out rooms to gentlemen and their paid company. Papa's room, the lanai, became the most popular one for its exotic qualities: wild flowers, wild air, wild sex. Diyosa used her blue-lit glow to seduce men of middle to old age, giving them her alabaster skin, her legs that lingered from toe to thigh, and her tresses that smelled like twilight's open blooms. At night, she was lady divine.

And there, at nightfall, I saw what they saw in her. But even more so, I saw what they didn't. Out and apart from the backdrop of the mansion, Diyosa kindled a different side of her being. I saw not a prostitute made beautiful by products, whose worth was determined by what she could give and do, but a lady making every square inch of space into a generous and intimate reception, a stage for her singing.

She took my bucket and began to pump. I said nothing and did not move. Certainly, I thought, they liked her, loved her, because compared to the other mistresses and whores, and to Mama who had become as strong as her tea and as stiff as her gin and tonic, Diyosa maintained an ease and a luminescence amidst the mansion's gloaming.

She filled my two containers and topped off hers, singing still as she smirked and gestured toward the direction of the mansion. We walked back together, our gallons of water in hand, her tune and tone taking the strain out of my eleven-year-old muscles. I had known no better way to walk home.

I asked her where she was from.

"Cebu, but I was born in Clark Air Base," she said.

Cebu was known as a fast-paced, tourist-heavy city, and Clark, an American airbase peopled by light-skinned, forgotten bastards of G.I. Joes like Norman, the product of an indigenous Abrenian laundrywoman and a soldier from New Jersey.

She continued on, half whispering and half singing her story. She told me that her mother worked on the base, visiting several Americans each night. With the number of pilots and privates she had slept with, there was no way of telling who Diyosa's father was. Her mother sent Diyosita to a parochial school, keeping her off the streets at least until the age of twelve. Her mother died of some undiagnosed illness, and the day after her mother's burial, Diyosa took after the only legacy she'd been left with—the art of making men happy. And there her transformation from Diyosita to Diyosa took place, aided by her half-American skin. Men prized and worshiped and adored it as the country did Our Lady.

On Monday, I arrived at school before sunrise, scrounged the grounds for leftover Coke bottles, and turned in my collection at the cafeteria, in exchange for a plate from the janitors' breakfast buffet: salted and dried threadfin fish. Then I went to the prayer room, sat cross-legged as I prayed the day's thanksgiving and requests. "Lord, thank you for my new friend. Please help me with today's civics exam. I did my best studying. Please keep me safe, fed, and strong for yet another day. Amen."

At the ring of the bell, I headed to my classroom, confident in my knowledge of history. While repeating names of Philippine revolutionaries to myself, a pea-sized ache jerked from my lower abdomen. It jerked and jerked until the ache was a full-on cramp, the kind I had had four months back—the week of my infested water ration. I sat down in my designated seat, assigned according to the first letter of our last names. My friend Bunny had left a bouquet of sharpened no. 2 pencils on the desk, perhaps aware of my limited resources and struggles at home. I turned around to find her in a classroom full of students, to thank her, but kept getting interrupted by the spasms. *Oh no,* I thought, *not again. I know I boiled the water, and I'm sure I kept the lids on. Oh no, Jesus, no.*

And then the wet feeling came. It spread through what felt like the entirety of my tattered underwear. *Oh no.* The test proctor handed me an exam. I wrote my name on the top corner, or at least tried to. The wetness kept increasing, dispersing itself past my undergarment, and soon, if I let it, through my skirt. I got up and ran out of the classroom. The proctor yelled, "Hey! Hey! You can't leave! Come back at once!"

I reached the bathroom stall, pulled down my skirt and panties, and slumped down to the toilet. It was not diarrhea. I wasn't sure whether I was grateful, knowing that I hadn't contracted yet another malarial-type bug. But there it was, reddish brown, brownish red, smeared on my underwear and marking my passage into another time: womanhood.

My mouth went dry. I looked up at the stall door to make sure it was locked and that nobody could walk in on my discovery. I thought of taking off my undergarment, wrapping it in toilet paper, and throwing it in the trash. But I realized that my menses would continue to flow, and I needed something to catch it. I pulled up my boy shorts from ankles to knees, rolled up a wad of toilet paper, and laid it over the stain. I crept out of the bathroom, sweating cold sweat, and shuffled my feet to the school clinic.

I came home wearing disposable underwear and a new skirt—both pockets stuffed with feminine pads to last me two days—all from the school nurse. I also came home with a permission slip from the principal, requesting my mother's signature for a retake of the exam that I, as the proctor had noted on the slip, "had evaded."

I wanted to tell Mama about my unwanted visitor, but she, as on any other day she spent at home, busied herself with magazines and periodicals in the breakfast room, while Norman drank coffee, whiskey, or both.

"Look here. This article says the coming election is the year of the newcomer. No more incumbents. Do you see what I see?" she said.

"I can always rely on your smart ass," Norman said, grabbing her face and kissing her hard on the lips. "Abra, I'm coming home with a vengeance! Last time I was there, I was the poor guy. This time I'll be the powerful guy. My people will be killing and getting killed for *me*."

Mama gave her nervous sniffs. Norman belched after stuffing a stale donut into his mouth. From where I stood under the arched entryway, I could smell the stink of his breath and the lack of showering wafting from under her arms. Mama's head bobbed from her undernourished body, and from her bun a gumamela flower stuck out. She had stopped washing herself because of the lack of water, but she continued to do her hair.

I turned around, repulsed by their conversation and the odor that now filled the breakfast room, and headed upstairs for a nap.

I laid my head on my pillow and felt the curve of the fork—my weapon—under the feathers. It brought back memories of Paolo striking forks when I slept. And I missed him. I wondered how a big brother would have reacted to the news of my first period.

Diyosa, who had been staying in one of the extra bedrooms, heard my steps, crossed the terrace between our two spaces, and came into my room. Without asking or saying anything, she started stroking my hair with her fingers and sang. At the end of her song, she said, "Why so sad, sweet angel?"

I kept my mouth closed and pulled the bunched-up wads of feminine pads from my pockets. Even though I was turned away from her and I couldn't see her face, I felt her smile.

"Oh my. What a big day it's been for you! Now what should we do to mark it? Hmm. I could give you a rose, but no, I don't have any. Or I could tell you all the crazy folk tales about womanhood handed down by my mother, but no, those aren't even true. Hmm. Well, what about my favorite, makeup and dress up?"

I perked up. Without saying a word, I hugged her around the neck, overtaken by my excitement. I used to help do Mama's face in the morning in her walk-in vanity, right after breakfast. I remembered how close I felt to my mother in that moment and how distant thereafter.

Diyosa walked me to her room, Papa's post–Gulf War habitation, where stacks of his yellowed ledgers and documents were still piled up against the wall. A cot lay in the middle of the room next to an upside-down biscuit tin that had been transformed into a dresser. On the make-shift dresser, Diyosa had arranged her trade's accoutrements: pocket mirror; flamingo-pink blush; violet, turquoise, and gold eye shadow; Revlon's Smoky Rose lipstick; and a plastic bottle of imitation perfume.

In her room, we made our complexion fairer, our cheeks rosier, and our facial angles more contoured. We listened to her battery-powered radio. We sang. We murmured words of quiet rivers and whispering winds. Diyosa crooned to her unborn child, and I to my would-be rescuer: Papa, Paolo, anybody. And as we harmonized, she showed me how to properly place a feminine pad on my underwear. She stripped the wax paper to reveal the adhesive strip, then stretched taut the band of fabric between the leg holes and set the pad, without wrinkling an inch of my boy shorts, right in the middle, at a position straighter than a twelve o'clock hand.

She spent the evening telling me about the importance of keeping clean and predicted my need of a third water container. She also handed me a stash of her unused feminine pads, ones she hadn't needed since becoming pregnant. She warned me of the dangers of becoming a woman.

"You'll need to protect yourself, your body. You are changing, blooming, becoming more fragrant. And if there's one thing I want for you that I wish someone had prayed for me, it's that you keep your fragrance bottled and that nobody unworthy would ever spill it."

I had no response. I looked at the perfume bottle on the upturned tin—a plastic vessel containing Diyosa's essence. *I wonder what my essence smells like,* I thought. And I thought many other things that hadn't occurred to me: peaks and troughs throughout my body—calves and ankles, hips and waist, baby breasts and the skin between.

The week of my first menstrual period, I paid little to no attention to school or my books. I visited Diyosa in her room as soon as I got home and spent the afternoon and evening there until right before her men came. On Tuesday, we powdered our faces, glossed our lips, brushed our hair, and listened to her radio. The music and the company took me back to jeepney joyrides, to slowdown and sway time in Paolo's van. On Wednesday, we snuck into Mama's basement closet and tried on her clothes, pretending to be belles and debutantes at

Mansion Royale. On Thursday, I showed her my keepsakes: Paolo's old Nintendo, which I pretended to power on and play, the handed-down Game Boy, pictures of me with Paolo and Papa, and Tiffany, Calbolite, and Rollerblade Barbie. I showed her my books, and she requested for me to read them aloud.

On Friday, I showed her where Tachio was buried.

"This is Our Lady and she watches over my baby brother," I said, making the sign of the cross on my heart. "He died on my birthday."

She said nothing and rubbed her belly.

I rubbed it, too, and made the sign of the cross on it, and said, "You'll be a good mama. He'll be lucky to have you."

"He?" she asked, grinning and forming dimples on her blushing cheeks.

"I think it's a boy. I *know* it's a boy, like Tachio." I wrapped my arms around her waist and kissed her belly. "I know you'll take care of him and give him a good life—because ghosts don't live in your body."

"What do you mean?"

"There's at least one ghost living in my mama's body. She changes back and forth. But you don't go back and forth."

Diyosa sighed. She took my hand and walked me out of the garden, up the grand staircase, and into my bedroom. She tucked me in bed, kissed my forehead, and said, "Thank you."

On Saturday, water day, I knocked twice and opened the door to her bedroom and found only the cot that lay in the middle of the room, the upturned tin, the pocket mirror, the flamingo-pink blush, the peacock-colored palette of eye shadow, and the Revlon stick. No bottle of perfume. No Diyosa. A note had been left leaning against the mirror and blush. Diyosa had composed a letter that said she needed to leave the mansion for a new life, and that she would continue to pray for me, especially the young woman I was becoming. She warned me of the harm that might come with my becoming an adolescent, but also advised me to stay hopeful for a way out. *Hope for both of us,* she wrote.

I stepped out of the room and closed the door behind me. I attempted to sing our song, but the words wouldn't come and the tune wouldn't form. Earlier in the week, my abdomen cramped as a rite of passage. Now my heart wrenched in pain. The twisting inside my chest choked the notes and the melody, expunging every verse about the river and the wind. I left Diyosa's things untouched, enshrined, in the space where, at separate times, she, Papa, and I had found refuge. Stored away in a bedroom we had called "extra," her belongings waited for her return. And I—I had other things to do. I had water to fetch, food to scavenge, books to read, monsters to fight, and another woman to get to know.

Myself. Alone.

Sleep Now

1998

I inspected for termites on weekends when Elma worked fourteen-hour shifts at the wet market. She'd been saving money to buy inventory with—goods for her sari-sari. Out of boredom, I knocked on walls and floors with my knuckles, listening for a hollow sound. My hand hovered over patches that resembled soft spots on a baby's head: wood that had morphed into eggshell.

Mama wasn't amused by my game.

"You learn these games from being with *those* people. We are important people, don't you remember?" she said, walking past me down the long dark hallway and scoffing while she clipped on costume earrings. "Please be done with your game before our guests arrive."

She didn't have to tell me. I knew to flee before the men arrived. The nuns next door cued me. *Gong, gong,* the convent bells rang. When the clock struck six, I ran upstairs—at least I tried to run—to my safe space, alone again, accompanied only by the swishing of curtains and the light from coils. I scampered in fear of the darkness below, like an ant hurtling away from a growing puddle. I chanted as I panted, "SOS. Save our souls. Save our souls."

I stopped at the landing. A hole in the corridor floor drew me to a halt. It gaped and faced the ceiling, mouth open wide and ready to swallow whatever or whoever neglected to hop over or step aside. The orifice could hold an adult-size thigh. The hole meant that the termites, which had lunched their way through the back-lot shanty, the basement walls, the ballroom arches and furniture, the long dark hallway's floorboards, and the lanai door, had made their way to my haven. I had no memory of slipping and jarring a foot or a knee through a soft spot on the floor. But there it was—a hollow space—which meant someone had been roaming where I thought I roamed alone. I swallowed my spit and scanned the corridor from end to end. I looked down through the crater and then stepped over it.

I went into my room, lay in bed, and read classics the librarian had loaned me indefinitely—*To Kill a Mockingbird*, *The Secret Garden*, and *The Giver*. But by my twelfth year on earth and my ninth in the mansion, even the magic of books had started to fade. It was not that their power had diminished, but that my ability to see wonder in the circus had begun to wane. Every breath, every turn of the page, had become a possible moment of surrender. I reread the same section twice, thrice, and by the fourth time, dog-eared it, and switched to another title. I fell asleep like that, with books dog-eared and left open around and on me. I dreamed of running and tripping, and startled myself to a state I then called "falling awake." I went in and out of consciousness, lids fluttering open and closed, the heat and humidity causing me to stir. I hovered in this state between sleepiness and sleeping.

I heard noises from downstairs: belching, chortling, mumbling. I heard jokes about taxes, commies, and the missus. I heard cards shuffling and being slammed down onto tabletops, and a battery-powered radio sputtering the local news and a jingle for Chiclets gum. I heard men, drunk and maudlin, serenading their call girls, whom I guessed were, like on previous nights I'd been spying, sitting or gyrating or panting on the men's laps.

I fell asleep again and then woke up again. I heard scuffling down below. *Uuunhh* and *thud* and *thunk* echoed from over there to right here, through the perfect acoustics of our house that was once as grand as a symphony hall. I could hear a number of men wrestle each other on the main floor. They kept at it until Mama said, "Who wants a tour of the mansion?"

Norman and Mama gave their guests a tour to view the house's good bones. The men walked through the arched entryways and under the puzzle of mirrors, their whores' arms hooked around theirs. They examined and prodded the architecture. They speculated its history. Mama played tour guide and boasted about the mansion's past: how it had been the venue of many champagne-toasting parties, the set for many films, the stage for the latest fashions, the site at which many business deals were made. She took them around the gardens, the ballroom, the disco, the breakfast room, the master bedroom, the lanai, and the bar, but never upstairs.

But that didn't mean they never came.

I entered sleep again.

Close to midnight, the air in my bedroom changed. The door parted and a breeze cut through, and the atmosphere went from simply being quiet to somehow being discreet, controlled, restrained: a secret. The dankness in the room filled with smells of whiskey and gin. I felt someone cross along the footboard of my canopied bed and along its side, but I remained unsure of whether I was dreaming. The midnight ghost waved the canopy aside and reached in. In mid-slumber, I felt his hot breath on my face. I heard sighs and rasps alternate with shushing and the jingling of a watch. Sheets first rustled, then lifted off the bed and off my legs. I still had the fork under my pillow, but in sleep could not motion my hands from my sides up to where I had kept my weapon. I only fathomed that the tracing up, down, and between my thighs, the finger snaking around my baby breasts, the caress on my neck and mouth were really happening when all the petting and playing was over.

I was caught in a death trance, running—and I'd never been a runner, but still, I tried. Pearl-and-oyster marble cemented my feet. My mind told my legs to move fast, fast, *faster!*

Keep the bottle closed, don't let your perfume spill. Run fast, fast, faster! Wake up!

My eyes opened, my sheets were moist.

And then nothing—nothing but darkness.

The next morning, I woke up and went straight to Diyosa's old room. I curled up in her cot and stared at her left-behind shrine: her upturned tin, pocket mirror, flamingo-pink blush, peacock-colored eye shadow, Revlon stick, and her farewell note to me. I crawled to her makeshift dresser and picked up the note and read it, read it again, then set it down between the mirror and blush. Then, as if warped out of time and thrown back in, I searched for her perfume bottle, forgetting that she had taken it with her. But I looked under the cot, felt around it, scoured around the perimeter of the room, looked inside closets, looked between stacks of yellowing paper, and peered through holes in the wall. I panted while I rifled, ransacking the room until I remembered that Diyosa was no longer there and neither was her essence.

And neither was mine.

I crossed the terrace back to my room and pulled Tachio's swaddle out of the drawer. I rolled it into a baby and cradled it. I patted its bottom, just as slightly and rhythmically as my yaya used to do to help me sleep.

"Shhh. Don't cry," I said, blowing gently onto its face. "I said don't cry! It's just milk—just spilled milk!"

I rocked it harder, swinging myself side to side so fast that the hem of my skirt lifted up into a parachute. "Shush! Stop crying! It's just spilled . . . spilled . . ."

Spilled perfume. I couldn't say it.

I went about my day with a stomachache and a side cramp and soreness in parts I would rather have ignored, parts I would rather have not had. I took Rollerblade Barbie, her clothes now all gone but her lighter skates still on, and plunged her into the ice-cream bucket of water to drown her. The skates stopped sparking, the fire quenched by my ration of stagnant water.

I abandoned books altogether. I refused love in this way. Instead I drew on Papa's old ledgers, heavy-inking over tally marks and net profits and claims. I etched bodies, hundreds of them, at times whole, but many times dismembered. I wrote my name over and over in curlicue calligraphy, then crossed out every *C*, every *I*, every *N*, every *E*, and every *L*. I dragged the black pen across my name, etching, engraving, lines through the letters with which my parents had christened me. I also wrote on myself—my thighs, my wrists, my palms. I impressed black over my birthmark, my stigmata, my Lucky Star. I drew *X*'s and *O*'s wherever I had an inkling of being touched. *XOXO*. Hugs and kisses. Death and dark wishes.

I spent time in Mama's garden, now barren of flowers and consumed by overgrowth. I sat where the orchids once bloomed, pretending to be a character from *The Secret Garden*. I talked to Tachio and brought him meals I refused to eat and left plates of rice and sardines on his grave, on the plot of dirt where his preterm body continued to decay. His perfect nose, his perfect lips, his ten fingers, ten toes, rotted away, bit by bit digested by maggots—his body having given itself as nutrient, as an offering, to dead soil.

I sang to him. "Happy birthday to you. Happy birthday to me. Happy birthday, dead baby. Happy death day, you and me."

I searched the grounds for the makahiya, shy plant, sleepy plant, sensitive plant, shamed plant, touch-me-not. I suspected that a clump of them hid underneath a fallen bougainvillea leaf. I waved the bougainvillea off with the back of my hand, reached for the makahiya's spine and traced it with my finger. I blew hot breath on its blades, snaked my pinky around every micro leaf, and watched it fold. It cowered into itself and away from me, the predator.

"Wake up!" I yelled at the fern.

It stayed clutched up.

"Wake up!" I yelled again and remembered that my yaya once told me that the makahiya closed around predators in the dark and reopened in the light. I bent down and kissed it. "I know."

I understood that plant—I knew its fear of nightfall. And I knew its longing for light.

I trawled myself through the damp air and back upstairs. I crumpled to the floor, next to the termite hole, and folded in. I stayed stock-still as if I were four years old again, on the concrete, my faculties unable—I had only my awareness. I recalled lying on the stretch of my parents' and brother's laps in the back of the car, my mother's wet hair and tears falling on and covering my face. I remembered hearing everything around me: my mother's weeping and nagging, my father barking at the help and making arrangements to save me and singing to me refrains about sunshine, and my brother repeatedly apologizing as he sobbed. I remembered not bleeding, not leaking red from my beat-up skull, not showing signs of trauma besides lying still, being unable to move, and, seemingly, deceptively, as only a kid can do, appearing tranquil.

Good night, mansion.

Good night, world.

I ambled to my room and rested on one side. Motionless, unable to speak, I hurt in places outside my body. I told myself to hurt no more because, perhaps, dying would drown me to the depths of darkness and through it, perhaps toward light. Perhaps a girl with curled fists, digging her nails into her palms, could show him, them, that they'd hurt me, killed me, as only a grown-up could do to a child.

Sleeping was dying; dying was sleeping.

Close your eyes.

Go to your room.

Go to bed.

Shush.

Good night.

The six o'clock bells rang. The sun was coming down now. I saw it ease from the top corner of my window and toward the sill. The black approached, encroached, surmounted over all that was and is and will be. But then, there it was, at the moment just right before dusk touched down—evening's blue light: Diyosa's glow.

In the blue light, peacock-colored eye shadow gleamed, moonflowers blossomed, the moon itself so coyly shone, and Our Lady—the blue-cloaked saint—stood watching over us with regal beauty and a peaceful face. In the blue light, the makahiya opened one last time before it slept to receive twilight's dew and the last rays of sun, the rays that signaled the promise of its return.

Gong, gong, the convent bells rang, reverberating, resounding, at six o'clock on the dot, the peace that I knew was meant for me, the peace that I knew as my own, the peace that knew everything: the petting, the playing, and the praying; the peace that knew my name. Those who roamed the mansion—they knew not this peace, this hand that reached out for me, ebbing, flowing, swishing, shushing, beckoning.

Sleep now and come.

Election Day

I had almost forgotten that I was in some kind of war when I woke up on the first day of summer break to Norman yelling, "Pulitika!" He raised a pistol and pointed it at the ceiling of mirrors in the ballroom.

"Pulitika!" Mama and their cronies said in return, also aiming arms at my sweet, spectacular glass puzzle above. I prayed they wouldn't fire and shatter it as I watched them from two arched entryways away, my fright disabling one muscle after another.

"Ah, there she is," Mama said as she slipped her pistol down into her last Hermès bag. She moved toward me in her signature high-heeled style. And as she always did to show contempt for my appearance, she exhaled heavily and brushed the hair off my face. "It's time."

I flicked her hand away. Her words brought hot blood out from some hidden segment of my marrow, and my face and ears reddened, my toes curled under, my tongue dried like salted cod in the hot sun. I shook my head.

"We're going north and spending the summer there," Mama said.

"No. Why would I want to go anywhere with you?" I said. "I'm staying in the mansion."

"Pack your bags or not, you're coming. We leave in an hour. You might even like it there."

"No."

"We are going north because we matter—*still* matter—there. The capital has nothing for us now. This mansion is crumbling, but we can build another one up there. Your grandfather ruled up north. I know the North. The North knows me. So today we go." She grabbed my arm, walked me out of the ballroom and up the steps, and said, "I am your grandfather's legacy. Now pack."

Narra, jackfruit, and mahogany trees, laden with dye-producing bark, leaf, and fruit, blazed our trail like a parade of welcome offerings. Yellow bursted more yellow, red gave way to deeper red, and green and brown bled into each other like brother and sister from an earthen mother god. Seeing light dispersed in this new fashion, I thought perhaps I'd been color-blind until now. Ten hours north of Manila, saplings grew uninterrupted, rice paddies spread, bamboo fenced houses, and pebbles scattered at the foot of colossal rock formations. Orange-bellied pitta and maya birds perched close to the highway, and rare shrews and Philippine deer roved into and out of the road, deciding the stop-and-go of our Land Cruiser.

How beautiful, how natural, this place called the North.

Cliffs made for roads, skirting us around mountain fringes. Tony drove the four-wheel drive with one hand on the steering wheel and the other clamped onto the gear, thrusting it forward and back, slight right and far right and left and center. Norman and Mama bobbed in the passenger seat while I flailed between bags and boxes in the cargo space. I held on to the assist handle and looked out the window. I followed egrets with my eyes and stretched my neck to see them fly from paddy to paddy. I traced rock formations on the glass window. I saw colors drip from woven blankets draped over clotheslines: umber, indigo, crimson, cobalt, saffron, and fire. Despite the rough ride, I enjoyed this new scene, this new space, this place that Norman called home and had described as captivating.

Cordillera, Cordillera.

At times the vehicle stopped, the engine unable to take the bash from the rocky road. Then once more we would resume our journey, the engine grunting. Again and again: stop, go, stop, go. And again and again: mountain, carabao, chicken, goat, tall tree, short tree, and then a man or woman in loincloth and feathered turban appeared and disappeared, rolling away before I could even name them.

And as we slowed after a kilometer-long stretch of undeterred speed, as if on cue, Norman said with uncanny sweetness, "Abra." In Spanish, meaning open—or, in this case, a clearing between mountains. The sound of the name rolling off Norman's tongue indicated that he was nearing home. He kept saying it. "Abra, Abra." He repeated the name as if to command the ridges to part, to give way and let us in, as if he were really saying, "Abracadabra."

The land listened and a river appeared. Tony turned off the engine, rolled down his window, clicked his tongue, and summoned four boaters to the side of the truck while handing them a twenty-peso bill. The stick-thin men motioned our vehicle onto a raft made of tied-up bamboo and several canoes. Instead of crossing a bridge, the Land Cruiser traversed from bank to bank on a rough-and-ready buoy. We floated on, bobbing along the forty-five-meter-wide river, trusting completely that a platform of sticks on a film-thin keel could bring us through the blue—from evergreen there to the evergreen yonder. *This* was the closest I'd been to a body of water. *Maybe I will like it here. Maybe this is better than the mansion*—my first thoughts of life outside, my first thoughts of escape.

Like Elma and I used to row with invisible paddles in our cardboard canoe, Norman and Tony high-fived each other and pointed at marvels near and far. "There! Look there! See!" They called out words in a northern dialect and met each advancing motion with glee. At the raft's first touch of land, Tony turned to Norman and shook his hand and said, "Welcome home, Gov."

We arrived at a place they referred to as a "safe house," an abandoned Spanish colonial home with a terra-cotta roof, half-hanging shutters, and a metal roll-up door—a cross between a romance-era carriage house and a storage unit. A man in military pants and a basketball jersey walked toward the Land Cruiser with his rifle hanging from his shoulder. "Gov," he said, saluting to Norman. He unlocked the metal roll-up door and pushed it up, banging on it once and saying, "Bulletproof." He smiled and gave me a thumbs-up.

The first floor contained about eight worktables—two-meter slabs of reclaimed wood on what looked like repurposed plumbing and bike parts welded together. From the floor rose towers of paper, new and old, printed and blank. Then next to them sat tin vats of rugby glue, and clay pots and glass jars of dye—the same reds, yellows, greens, and browns from the trees that had blazed our trail to this place.

We walked up a spiral staircase made of the same metal as the door. On the landing stood and squatted about thirty armed men in military pants and shirts that appeared to have been rummaged from Goodwill. They scattered throughout the second floor, some jeering with each other, some smoking, some looking out and guarding windows, but all at attention to whatever or whoever occupied the front of the room. I walked behind Norman and Mama, while Tony and his men tailed behind with our suitcases and crates of guns. The crowd parted wherever we stepped, saluting and giving thumbs-up, their congeniality serving as some affirmation, some warmth, some flesh, some soul, in the midst of silver and steel.

Then there, there he was.

"Father," Norman and Mama said, reaching to shake his hand.

The man set down his tin cup, got up, brushed off biscuit crumbs from his army pants and white polo shirt, and shook their hands. "Welcome, comrades, Ka Norman and Ka Estrella." Then he turned to me and made the sign of the cross on my forehead, as priests did for children.

"Father Balweg, finally, we are together. You, your militia, us, and our team—we will win Abra. We will govern it and make it ours again. We will win it back for the people of the Cordillera," said Norman, scanning the room. I had heard of the name Balweg—Conrado Balweg. I'd seen him on the news and in chapters preceding the appendix of history books. No doubt, the man who just anointed my forehead was the same rebel priest who led the Cordillera People's Liberation Army, a heavily armed communist guerilla group from the Tingguian tribe of the North. Mr. Santiago talked about him in class.

"Post-Spanish, post-American, post-Marcos, post-Aquino, post–Pope John Paul II," Mr. Santiago had said. "We are living in the most dangerous of times. Why? Because of new armies led by men like Conrado Balweg. And because of their weapon: *children.*"

My heart started to beat faster.

Norman bragged to Father about each one he had brought with him, me included. And then it clicked: I understood why the Common Enemy had come here and why he had come into our lives. I had learned about this at the library and in another one of Mr. Santiago's classes.

"There are seven *M*'s to building a dynasty," Mr. Santiago said. "Money, machine, media, marriage, murder, myth, and mergers."

Each one of us, from Mama and me to Tony and his men—we were Norman's seven *M*'s. He managed an eighth one, too—*M* for mansion. He returned to the Philippines after having lived a life in California and New Jersey, in hopes of running for office and building an empire of some malicious sort. The day he met Mama at the Hotel InterContinental, the moment he heard her maiden name and made sense of her breeding and belongings, he knew he had caught the wildest catch—a mestiza daughter of an Ilustrado with a background in politics, unraveling from her multi-million-dollar marriage, living in a pearl-and-marble palace, and raising a child who was supposedly good at writing speeches and speaking to the masses. The only thing we couldn't give him was murder—the trigger-happy militia. And so he coalesced with one widely feared man, revered both at church and on the battlefield, and whose men could fashion an M16 out of scrap metal from an old ship. Norman had lost his home in Jersey, so now he was to reclaim his home in the mountains—his birthplace and that of his late mother's, his mother who fed him scraps from the seminary kitchen. I'd heard him talk of the poverty he grew up in, but only now could make sense of the bitterness in his heart. He grew up in a province where bridges didn't exist, where cars floated on makeshift rafts, where American privates and missionaries impregnated women and abandoned them, where indigenous people tended rice terraces unclothed and unprotected from storm and sun, where industry was controlled by 3 percent of the population, where foreign aid was distributed among the rich and not the needy, where the hateful advised the powerful, and where clergy and commanders shook hands with Communists.

"Laban! Laban ng Makabayang Masang Pilipino!" the room roared. Fight! Fight of the Nationalist Filipino Masses!

They pounded their rifle stocks against the floor. I quivered to the beat. I perused the room to look for my mother, who intoned with their incantation, her manicured hands beating the air in rhythm with their chapped, calloused, bandaged, knuckle-heavy fists. Her last pair of Dior heels, red like blood and like her nails, *click-clack*ed against the same floor the goons' duct-taped boots plodded. It was as if all the chapters from the history books I had read had somehow folded into one—Tribal Times and Prehistory, Indigenous Cultures, The Kingdom of Tondo, The Rajahnate, The Sultanate, The Bruneian Empire and Rise of Islam, The Spanish Era and Catholicism, The Philippine Revolution of 1898, The American Era, The Commonwealth, The Marcos Era and Martial Law, Communist Insurgence, The People's Revolution, The Rise of the Tiger and the Asia-Pacific Economic Cooperation, The Fifth Republic. What next?

We are living in the most dangerous of times.

The most dangerous of times.

Danger.

Common Enemy.

Why? Because of the new weapon—children.
Weapons of destruction.
Silver and steel.
Children.

There was nothing on TV except coverage of the elections. For the first time in years, we had power and a working antenna, and what a let-down it was to flip from channel to channel, only to find rosters for politicos and supporters already bludgeoned to death by their warlord counterparts. On the bottom-left corner of the screen flickered an ongoing counter, ticking away digit by digit, going up from the tens to the hundreds in no time. Each digit represented the number of casualties and wounded military, paramilitary, and civilians. The camera panned to a blown-up car on the side of the road some twenty miles from the safe house, showing four bodies burnt from the midsection up.

The news reporter said, "And the bloodbath continues as political clans war against each other."

Election Day was still a month out.

Both startled and bored, I went down the spiral steps to kill time on the first floor. I had always been fascinated by handiwork, so the vats of glue and pots of dye were of interest to me. I traced my finger around the mouth of each vat and pot and stirred the bamboo sticks resting in them. I sniffed the reams of paper soaring from the asphalt floor and flipped through the corners as if they were the edges of my dearly beloved library books. I stepped over rifles to get to every inch of the room, picking up and examining, feeling rulers, paintbrushes, and gauze.

Then a ringing sound came from the other end of the room. I looked up. Norman was tracing the rim of a dye jar with his finger, making a pinging sound. He stopped to point his finger at the paintbrushes.

"Interested, huh? All my savings have gone into guns and this. And you'll get to play with these things. Lots."

"What do you mean?"

"I want you to go outside and find some friends. Bring 'em back here and tell 'em you have a little art project you need help with. Go. Dinner depends on it."

Norman ushered me out the back door. I stepped out, one flip-flop at a time, scouting the grounds for these so-called friends. Immediately, two boys came into sight and rushed out of the bushes. They first spoke in their dialect, then guessed by my lack of response that I only knew Tagalog—Manilagirl, that particular kind. I gave them my age, told them where I went to school, who I came with, and what I liked to do. And all they said, in Tagalog, was "Want to play?"

I smiled with my eyes and the shorter one tagged me.

I had never been a runner, but the fact that I was among children who knew nothing about the mansion and who cared little to nothing about where I was from made me sprint to tag the next It. I had never been a runner, and yet was thrilled to be part of the game.

Once tag got old, we moved on to other diversions: tumbang preso (knock down the prisoner), patay-patayan (playing dead), agawan base (stealing base), langit lupa (heaven and earth), and ubusan ng lahi (wipe out the clan)—games that our adult counterparts seemed to be playing and *enjoying* at a different level.

The sun started to set and I still hadn't employed the help of my new friends. Dinner depended on it, I remembered.

"Hungry?"

The set of them, now a group of eight barefoot, tatter-dressed boys and girls between the ages of seven and fourteen—and cumulatively weighing about 275 pounds—countered, "In exchange for what?"

"My stepfather has a project for me and I need help," I said, as if certain of the task at hand.

"Using dye?"

"Lots of dye."

"We know dye. We are from the Tingguian tribe and our mothers and grandmothers make dye."

"Perfect. So who's ready for dinner?"

We frisked along: hungry children, lonely children, children ready to work for a bite or two.

We arrived at the safe house and entered through the back where Tony and a few men smoked and chewed tobacco. Tony nudged the guerilla boy next to him, who was about fifteen, who then reached under his Monobloc plastic chair and pulled out a plastic bag of Styrofoam containers. He held it out to me, the leader of my newly formed pack, and gestured for me and my troupe to eat. I set the bag on the floor and opened it. My friends waited as I popped each top. We gasped every time the contents of each of the four containers were revealed. They gasped in excitement, and I gasped in revolt. They called the first dish abuos, a stir-fry of giant red ant eggs. The second dish they called abal-abal, vinegar-dressed beetles. The third they called kampa, a white fish found only in the Abra River and boiled in tamarind soup. The fourth they had no special name for but looked the most familiar to me: rice. So I let them have a go at the first three dishes, while I took a fistful of the long grains. Within five minutes, the food was gone.

Tony unrolled a poster and flattened it out on one of the worktables. He pointed at it, then to a crumpled sheet with handwritten lettering and said, "Copy these words but make it look like this," referring to the poster. The poster read "ERAP PARA SA MAHIRAP!" Erap for the poor! Erap was the name of a former actor running for president. On the sheet, someone had spelled Norman's and Father's names, along with a caption about serving the underprivileged and the indigenous, and the titles "Gobernador" and "Bise Gobernador." I drafted a mock-up, copying the sheet's text, but in the typestyle, color, and size as on the poster. Tony, his men, and the kids watched over my shoulder as I drew and erased, drew and erased. At the fourth try, I did it—I made a master copy of Norman's election posters. The armed men and the now not-so-hungry children clapped for me. I felt hot around my neck and the back of my ears. I blushed. I felt proud of myself, but also ashamed and angry—knowing that my art was to aid Norman in reaching his dream of being in office. I imagined him rebuilding another mansion, hiring more men, and enlisting more children. I thanked the group for their praises, in the softest, tremulous voice I could speak in because I couldn't help but think of what Mr. Santiago had said. *The most dangerous of times. Danger. The new weapon—children.*

I also knew that my sketch and calligraphy were only the beginning.

The kids and I spent after-dinner hours silk-screening my design onto letter-size and tabloid-size sheets. After we'd gone through the stacks of paper around the room, Tony unboxed cotton T-shirts for us to tint with dye. Our little hands worked like cogs and bolts in a printing press, Norman's version of a campaign and a political machine. I thrived in the rhythm of this new game—press, pour, push, pull, push, pull, print. I gave directions and the kids listened, not because I was the oldest, but because my education and class gave me a sense of command. As a leader, I felt the need to protect my legion, to make sure that what Mr. Santiago said—*danger*—would never meet my troupe.

"I need to go home," the shorter one said.

"We still have work to do," I said.

"But my mom will think that I joined an army."

"What army?" I asked, setting down my dye stir stick.

"Goons for the mayor or governor. *Bang-bang.*"

"*Bang-bang?*"

"My cousin Chito, who's twelve, has joined. My brother and I have been asked. Chito cuts grass now, but soon he'll have a gun, too." He pretended to fire.

I sent them all home and asked them to return first thing in the morning. "There will be breakfast," I assured them. I commended them for the meticulousness of their little sweatshop hands, their head-down-mouth-shut work ethic, their listening skills, their speed and agility, and even how well they ate their food. I gave them endless praise—to lure them back to *my* army and not anybody else's. The silk-screen work, it stung and stained our skin, but better the sting of dye than the pouring of blood.

Morning broke and I roused to the memory of last night's conversation. *Goons for the mayor or governor. Bang-bang.* I ran to Norman and Mama's sleeping quarters, where they sat up in bed reading the paper, so I could ask for a ration of bread and condensed milk for the kids coming to help me that day. Mama said that Tony had gone to pick up a brown bag of pan de sal and should be back shortly, and that asking for condensed milk was asking for too much, and that we should get printing done by midday so we could hang the posters up all over town by dusk. I left without responding, hurrying to get clothes and flip-flops on, and scurrying down the spiral steps to await my troupe. I prayed, "Oh, God, please bring them here and not there." I thought of the inscription etched on the private school's chapel doors: "Let the little children come to me." Over and over I prayed, hands clasped and teeth grinding, breathing shallow breaths just down and into my shoulders and nowhere past. *Where are they?*

The back door opened and Tony walked in.

"Your gang's here. They followed me from the panaderia. They can smell bread from a kilometer away, these little scamps. Feed them bread and get to work."

I brought my prayer hands to my lips, sighed, and whispered, "Thank God for bread."

Sponges slid against mesh from morning till noon. The kids and I inked enough paper and cotton to dam the Abra River, then Tony paid us with lunch plus a couple bottles of Coke. Sugar streamed in our blood; our fingers stung, our grins stretched from ear to ear. Tony packed us into the Land Cruiser and drove us into town, where we were to hang up posters.

The T-shirts, he said, were to be given out the day of the motorcade rally. Still glucose-manic, my band and I hastened through the municipality, gluing paper to walls and posts, onto wooden planks, bamboo fences, and corrugated tin, covering the town with Norman's ballyhoo. As the verve wore off, my breath slowed. Out of things to post, my body knew not what to do in a town that wasn't my own. So I watched.

Warty pigs, stray dogs, chickens, dwarf palms, and cartfuls of green bananas lined the street. Potholes sank into areas touched by cement, and where the paving ended, grit spread. Children squatted on the sidewalk, writing in the dirt with rocks and sticks and breathing the dusty air rising from the ground. Half of them wore shorts and nothing else. Motorcycles zipped past, dodging the zigzag of chicks and children by a hair. I was close to thinking that Abra was much like Manila—poor people scattered here and there. But then I thought to look again, to squint and see what might really be.

Guns.

Villagers had pistols slipped into back pockets while the Tingguians tucked them into their loincloths. Motorcyclists rode with one hand on the clutch and the other curled around a trigger. Men playing cards shuffled their decks with a gun muzzle, while prepubescent boys sitting at their feet shined the spare. And on the dirt path, three- and four-year-olds hopscotched over silver shells. Abracadabra. Open. Open fire.

The mountain region decked itself with bush and bandit; I could hardly decide what kind of wilderness Mama and Norman had taken me to.

A mansion, similar to ours in size and shape, towered over the outback and the rice terraces. On the side of the mountain it hung, spangled and taunting the dearth of village life.

"Valera clan," the shorter one of my original two playmates informed me.

"Who?"

"Governor of Abra. Many years. Long time."

"That's who Norman is running against? That's the army you were talking about?"

He pulled out his imaginary gun one more time. "Yes. *Bang-bang*.
Bang-bang for jobs, bang-bang for money, bang-bang for land, for food,
for goat, for chicken. You not serve Valera, you not eat. You die. You—
you and family—crazy."

"You could say that," I said, exhaling. "Now how do I get out of it?"

He shrugged. "No way out. We all too hungry."

I thought of what Papa once said: *People only band together when they
have a common enemy.* The villagers and the Tingguians banded together
because they lived in an impoverished, isolated part of Luzon. Tony and
the men who had been living in the mansion fixed their hope on the
next guy who promised change because there were no jobs in the Middle
East, no jobs in the provinces, and no jobs in Metro Manila. And now
the commies were doing the same: they were committing themselves
to the next new thing, say, a half-American man from New Jersey, with
truckloads of guns and goons, trailed by rumors of a mansion and money
elsewhere, and a wife who resembled the Virgin Mary.

This was our Common Enemy: death by hunger.

"Boss Tony is calling," the shorter one said. "Time to go."

The Land Cruiser brought us back to the safe house, where about forty
had gathered. Tingguians, commies, children, Tony's men, Norman, and
Mama sat around a campfire—a scene so foreign, I had to be startled out
of stock-stillness with a beat of a gong. Gangsa, the Tingguians called it. I
jolted every time they beat it. The banging took me back to a time when
Paolo and I played army, when I had thrown a baby-powder grenade over
a fort of pillows—our talcum bomb exploding on the top floor, he and
I cackling at the destruction we had caused. The tribesmen flitted to the
music, amplifying the tune with the swish of feathers tufted from their
turbans. The women and children clapped to the beat, and the commies
pounded their gunstocks against the ground. The louder they got, the
more nervous I felt.

Dizzying, dizzying, falling.

"You," Norman summoned. "Inside."

He and Mama led me through the back door and up the spiral steps. Mama spoke as she walked. "I've done such a great job with you: smart, strong, resourceful. They said you would never make it, and yet here you are, running a campaign with me. Now what we need is for you to write a speech. Write us something convincing."

"Don't fuck this up, Strong Will. I didn't come back to this godforsaken place to get screwed over. I'm here to win. And you're here to help me. And if we succeed, you might even get a weekly allowance," Norman said. "Now get to work."

They left me at the landing where I had met Father Balweg earlier that week.

As they walked away, I whispered, "I will fuck this up, Norman. Like you fucked us up."

I sat on a gun crate, next to a desk with a pen and paper, and wrote by lamplight all that I knew. I knew that people from my class had hurt people below us, and that my people remained at their stations because others chose to devote their lives to our service. I knew that when my parents lost everything, it was Elma and her family who'd chosen to protect me, to feed me, to teach me, and to be my kin. I knew that the children of Abra were at stake, as my friend, the shorter one, had tried to tell me.

And there, by lamplight, I penned an apology to the people of Abra and asked for forgiveness for a multitude of sins: for the starvation and poverty, the lack of bridges and fully paved roads, the need for guns and hypervigilance, and for the danger their sons faced daily.

I wrote with my pen: "This man you are about to vote for, he is not a nice man. I've seen him do things. He's brought my home and my family down. He will bring you down, too."

The speech lived in my skirt pocket overnight. Mama and Norman so trusted my skills that they didn't think to review what I had written. All they asked was that I get in the cargo space of the Land Cruiser after breakfast and travel with them on convoy to the gubernatorial debate. We trucked on, ten beat-up autos of varying degrees of dent and rust, our ride fourth in line. Norman and Mama bobbed in their seats, and I thrashed back and forth: a replay of our trip to the North, but this time with bags of silk-screened shirts and posters around me. I had gotten used to this skid-and-go, and then—

Stop. A band of motorcycles and goons T-boned our motorcade.

"Stay in the car! Stay down!" Tony yelled and stepped out of the truck. He fired his gun toward the squad.

"Anak ng puta!" Norman said. He reached for his gun, rolled down his window, and blasted at the barricade of armed men.

"Stay down," Mama said as she grabbed me by the collar, pressing my face down on the floor mat. The mat's polyester purls scraped my cheek and the corner of my mouth, giving me a taste of my own blood. Mama let go of me, knowing I wouldn't dare get up. She half opened the door, hunkered behind it, reached into her Hermès bag for her gun, and blindly fired at the masks and motorcycles four cars from us—her manicured hands flailing in the wind with a weapon about a fourth of her weight. She yelled her favorite word, "Puñeta!"

I crammed my body under the back seat and screamed, "Mama! Stop! Stop! Papa, help!" I couldn't hear myself. The sound of silver on steel and steel on silver overpowered my cries. Bullets struck the tin around me until they lodged in bags of cotton—my friends' handiwork absorbing the blasts from the goons outside. I wanted to peek out the window to see where Mama was—*Was she safe? Okay? Alive?*

Craning my neck to look out the rear window without moving up from the mat, I searched for the colors and animals that had amazed me upon arrival. I saw pitta and maya birds fleeing from the scene, beating their baby bijou wings—gems lucky enough to have the gift of flight.

I did not have wings, so I made myself shrink. I curled my extremities under me. And I tried to sing my papa's song about sunshine and gray skies leaving. But again, my tongue dried like salted cod in the hellish Abrenian sun. So I tried monosyllabic words.

"Stop."

"God."

"Stop."

"Help."

"Stop."

The land listened. The shooting ceased.

I exhaled and turned to look out from under the seat. The rear window framed the shift in hue. Yellow paled. Green and brown turned into granite, as if camo and tree bark could be absorbed back into metamorphic rock formations. And red gave way to deeper red.

To red. To red. To red.

To blood black.

Tony suffered a gunshot wound to his ankle, leaving Norman to drive. He and Mama got back in the truck unscathed, saying nothing as we drove off. We overtook the three cars preceding us in the convoy—a slaughter of commies bleeding from multiple wounds. My scratched face stung as I looked back at the carnage: boys no older than Paolo swimming in pools of almost black, some with their legs still straddling fallen-over motorcycles and others slumped over another dead boy's body. I did not know which to cover with my dye-stained hands: my bleeding cheek or my eleven-year-old eyes.

At the roundabout, we U-turned to the safe house, never making it to the gubernatorial debate. The speech continued to live in my skirt pocket. It never reached the ears of those whose lives I'd hoped to somehow change. We arrived at the metal-and-terra-cotta building, where boys had been waiting to help us unload the crates and carry Tony in. Nobody made a sound except for Tony, who was moaning in pain. The boys gripped onto his limbs like the ends of a stretcher, and heaved

him up the spiral staircase. Norman followed, then Mama and me. I
sat down on the crate by the desk, and Mama sat on the sofa where she,
Norman, and Father Balweg had been drinking earlier that week. Mama
cried and I watched her. I watched her face turn red, her forehead and
hands turn veiny, her cheeks and neck get wet with tears.

"Stop crying and make yourself useful," Norman said to her, pointing at Tony.

She tried to control her sobs, but couldn't. Still, she attended to their
right hand, shaking as she tried to recall how to fix a nonfatal gunshot
wound. She asked one of the boys for his T-shirt and tied it around
Tony's leg as a tourniquet. Then she asked for Norman's whiskey, poured
it into the wound, and gave Tony some to drink. I watched Mama be a
doctor again. She hadn't been in the medical field since the Gulf War,
since she lost her medical license. And she hadn't been a nurturer since
Tachio's birth and death, so I found it oddly comforting to watch her
care for a human being. Perhaps the bloodbath was what we needed—
the U-turn at the roundabout as our way back to normal times.

Election Day came, and Norman lost. He said nothing in response to
the message of the gunfight. The kids I'd commissioned and played with
didn't turn up at the safe house again. All I could do was think of them
and pray for them, willing with my heart and gut that they hadn't joined
either army. Father Balweg and those of his men who hadn't died in the
cross fire returned to the boondocks, and we returned to Manila. Balweg
and his Cordillera men took their guns and gongs, leaving us as a failed
political machine with nothing but inked T-shirts and tattered posters.
The Land Cruiser crossed the river one last time on a bamboo raft: from
evergreen there to evergreen beyond, the rush of water underneath swishing us onward and away from the mountains and highlands, telling us
to never return to its killing fields again.

Monsoon Manifesto

1999

Someone was crying and it wasn't me. The sobs and sniffs kept coming, rippling from the terrace through the stale upstairs air. At first I thought it was my spirit, that perhaps it finally had departed from my frail body after the cross fire in Abra, and that it was wandering around like a ghost child looking for its mother's apparition or body. But my bones remained above earth, unhidden, woven still, and able to take shape like a fetus in the womb.

My pulse, her pulse. My pulse, her pulse.

Mama.

I moved. My fingers unfurled once, twice. I uncoiled from the fetal position, found a base for my weight on the elbow touching the mattress, then pushed up, strength by strength, until I sat upright and could swing my legs to the side of the bed. I let my body, hollowed of its purity, ache forward to the weeping at the terrace. I found my mother.

Mama bent over the banister, leaning so far out—a tiptoe away from a forward fall. She wore a shift dress and a robe, the kind she had on at breakfasts of years ago. It certainly didn't fit the weather predictions for the day—stormy with gusty winds. Her dress whipped against her now-veiny legs, and her robe sleeves billowed out around her arms.

Her hair flew around her face, like her hand and gun flailing in the
wind at the cross fire.

The sky hung full-bellied above us as strands of light flickered to
touch ground. From where we stood, we could see the nuns cart in
chairs and potted plants from the convent's garden. We watched as the
farmer and his sons hauled up grains into their shed. Pedicab drivers
took on an extra passenger for each route, clearing the sidewalks of
people before she came—La Niña. The girl.

"Mama?" I said.

She shook in her robe.

"Mama, the storm's coming. Let's go inside." I thought of reaching
for her hand.

"We have to go," she murmured, staring out into a foggy, faraway
world.

"Yes, we have to go. Let's go inside."

"No, we have to go. Now. Leave. He's gone. He's looking at chickens. Now."

The clouds echoed and urged us, and they thrummed.

"Okay, okay," I said. "Let's go. Quick."

Mama and I each ran to our bedrooms as it began to teem down.
We swiped things into bags within reach. I took books, of course, the
most dog-eared ones, and slipped a notebook, a pencil, my doll Tiffany,
Rollerblade Barbie, pictures of me with Papa and Paolo, and a few
skirts, shorts, and shirts, but left my school uniform, thinking that
leaving the mansion meant leaving my school. I left the fork under my
pillow, as I expected no need for it outside the world that my parents
had built. Goodbye, fork. Goodbye, *life*.

I clutched my duffel bag under my arm and ran out of the bedroom. I slalomed down the corridor, the way Milo and I used to do,
avoiding termite holes that had increased in number since our time in
Abra.

I met Mama at the main doors, not stopping to take a breath or to look back. We reeled forward in the rain, onward, down the driveway. "The van," she said, pointing to Paolo's old ride. She got in the driver's seat and I in the passenger's, stowing with us our salvages from Mansion Royale and dripping in our seats—soaked from rainwater and tears.

"Mama, I didn't know you could drive."

"We can learn anything just by watching. We can do anything, remember that. Forget everything, but remember that."

At the turn of the key in the ignition, she became strong again. The weeping stopped and the escape began. I jumped out of the car to unlock the gate, one *uunnnkk uunnnkk* at a time, just as I used to do before each cab route with Paolo. I hopped back in and we drove off, speeding away at ninety-six kilometers per hour, rushing out through the mansion's clearing before the Pacific rain flooded again.

Mama gritted her teeth and stepped on the gas, thrusting all her force down her right leg. I buckled in and reached down for the glove compartment, wondering if Norman had trashed Paolo's joyride treasures. But no, he hadn't. Perhaps he had never found them. Or he had discovered them and liked them. Under an unloaded gun and gum wrappers hid the soundtrack to glory days shared with my brother: mixtapes. A side, B side, it didn't matter. I slipped one into the stereo's mouth and waited for it to give its magical hiss before spewing out songs from happier hip-hop days: "Mo Money Mo Problems," "Tha Crossroads," "No Diggity," "Breakdown," "The World Is Yours," "The Most Beautifullest Thing in This World," and last on the track, "Gangsta's Paradise." I fanned out the rest of Paolo's stash and brought them to my nose and mouth, smelling the smell that captured a richer part of our childhood: plastic and chrome film. I cradled them, holding the weight of emotion and memory spooled around the tape reels. Mama cried while driving, and I cried, heaved, equally blue and blessed, taken by the music—my brother's soul and his very spirit.

Wherever we're headed, this is what we take with us, I thought. *Love in the memories. And many, many ghosts.*

We parked outside Excellz, Mama's old gym, where she used to take aerobics classes, and waited for a familiar face to walk out. Her old friend, named Linda or Minda or Ming, whose child was kidnapped and blinded by a local syndicate, came out of the building. She stood at the valet, waiting for her driver to pull up. Mama stepped out of the van and ran to her, shocking the woman with her informality and appearance: her thinning hair, chipped teeth, and sodden garments. Mama held her hands in prayer, pleading for something—I couldn't hear. The woman shook her head, more frantically as Mama continued to plea. Then Mama pointed my way. They looked at me through the rain and the fogged-up windshield, the woman cupping her mouth and nodding. I must have reminded her of her long-lost daughter.

Mama got back in the van, started the engine, and followed the woman's Mercedes. We trailed behind her in the deafening and vision-skewing rain, hunching over the dashboard and squinting to not lose track. After passing through two checkpoints, we entered an exclusive gated community and parked outside a house half the size of ours, but as majestic and shiny as the mansion had once been.

"We're sleeping here tonight," Mama said, shifting the gear to park.

"At her house? In these clothes?"

"No, outside. We're parking here and sleeping here. Now change into something dry while we wait for a maid to come out. She said she'd have a meal sent out to us."

"We're going to live in the van?"

"We have nowhere else."

"But . . . we can look for Papa. Or Paolo and his dad. Or maybe you have other friends who'd let us live inside . . ."

"Stop! I have nobody, so you have nobody," she said.

"You don't have anyone, but I do. Paolo loves me. He's just taking his time to get well. Papa will get back on his feet and get me. I know it! You have no one, but I do! They left *you*, not me!" I said, yelling at my mother who'd progressively shrunk from five foot big to five foot small.

She murmured with her forehead and hands on the steering wheel, her muttering rumbling within the walls of her wet hair. "I'm sorry, but please shut up now, please."

I crawled to the back of the van, changed into fresh clothes, and read. The food came and I ate, while Mama refused the meal and continued to sob. Her weeping and the ceaselessness of the rain befell and became our song for the night. I read and then slept.

I woke up to a break—moonlight assuaging the cadence of the rain and Mama's crying. Mama let up for a minute, then opened her door and ran out. She left the door wide open, so I crawled to it and jumped out. The rain hadn't eased and I couldn't see.

"Mama! Mama!" I yelled, running barefoot. I couldn't find her, but kept at it, running in a circle and trying to detect any semblance of my mother: her form, her scent, or the sound of her sobs or close-lipped singing. Then moonlight grazed the ground once more and led me to a smallness, a shape, the profile silhouette of her high-bridged nose, and the rest of her, quivering.

"Mama, let's go back inside the car," I said, this time reaching my hand out for hers.

"I want to dance," she said.

"Mama, it's raining hard and it's dark out. Please, let's go. Take my hand, Mama."

She grabbed my hand. And she twirled me.

"Mama, what are you doing?" I said as she swung my arm forward and back in a series of half circles—my lips hesitant but slowly curling into a smile.

She said nothing and kept dancing, tiptoeing from puddle to puddle, finally letting go of me and enjoying herself in the rush of adrenaline and the pour from the sky. The clouds kept giving and she kept receiving, arms wide open like a *Hallelujah!* to her second baptism, in the name, not of the Father or the Son or the Holy Ghost, but of La Niña.

"No more!" she yelled. "Goodbye, mansion! Goodbye, Norman! Goodbye to this fucking life! Puñeta kayong lahat!" Fuck you all.

The storm accompanied her declaration, inclining me to join in on this newfound manifesto.

"No more! Goodbye!" I said, dancing and twirling, this time not under a puzzle of mirrors, but an overhead sea of bursting crystals—a kaleidoscope in a black night.

We chorused. "We will build a new home—with electric power! With water! With food! All you coños can go to hell!"

"I hope you die, Norman!" Mama exclaimed. "Puñeta!"

"Puñeta!" I echoed my mother's favorite word.

She said it again with her arms held up as if to catch a rain cloud, her legs flitting about, her body windswept, and her dress falling off one shoulder and exposing a breast. And we laughed.

Laughter became our new refrain.

But as the winds grew stronger and the storm wilder, I thought it best to run back to the van. I reached out for Mama's hand again, inviting her to take shelter with me. But she kept dancing, losing herself to the gales of La Niña.

I stayed and I watched: my mother, the tempest, the prevailing wind.

As my eyes beheld her every move, I gave requiem to the things I had seen: Aqua Net hair. Unfinished house. Ten bedrooms. A garden party. Pistachio shells. Goblets of wine. Towers of champagne. Rollerblade Barbie with lighters for skates. Swollen ankles. A dead baby. A wailing woman in the moonlight. Stars. Orion's belt. A gold mirror and red lipstick. Heels against pearl-and-oyster marble. *Stay out of the sun. Too dark.* A crinoline petticoat dress. *Those ignorant and superstitious people.* The masses bowing down, a sea of them. Swan diving into the pool in her red Valentino one-piece swimsuit. Me falling, my body paralyzed. Her hair in my face. Jade urns. A crater. A knife in hand and my father running. Away. Still. White rattan peacock chair. Orange peel and ripples around a tea bag. Anaïs Anaïs. Her fingers leafing through *Vogue* and *Elle*. Magazines. Books. Words. Prêt-à-porter! Recherché! She's gifted! I kept you alive! The basement for a closet. Little black dress. Little brown girl looking up at her mother, dancing. Orchids in the garden. Coins in a Crayola coin bank. Makeup in the built-in organizer. Primer, powder, bronzer, and blush. Mr. Albrando. Tassels. Twirling beneath a kaleidoscope ceiling. Twirling the spindle on the Rolodex. Debutantes and belles. Dancing. Swirling. A flood. Floodwater throughout and through-in. Aerobics shoes, Dior heels, workout videos. Filling the air with her fast laugh and cocking her head back at a quick joke. Keys jangling. Motor running. A car door opening. A brown bag with a yellow chick inside. My dead Tweetie. Cockfighting. Animals disappearing. Animals dying. Shit everywhere. Children everywhere. Guns everywhere. Red nails and commies. *Bangbang.* Her manicured hand pushing my face down on the floor mat. Her manicured hand flailing in the wind with a gun. A shower of bullets. Of perfume spilled.

The rain.

My mother, dancing and breaking into a million memories—a million raindrops. A whole world in every tear. Breaking. Falling from the dark clouds, dripping, plummeting, plopping against my skin and vanishing at once.

I was drowning in a monsoon of her.

Not Water, but Whiskey

1999

Norman fell apart without Mama—or *me*—around. He didn't know his right fist from his left, his chicken-petting fingers from his key-tossing, ass-grabbing, gun-firing ones. Without a child to torment and another adult to blame, he could not withhold love, pour out wrath, and feel like an inhuman being. Without another's flesh, his flesh could not be pleased; his filth could not morph into disease. He begged us to come back.

"Water! There's running water!" He pulled strings and sold chickens and lured Mama with his promises and pleas. "Power, a full pantry, even cable!" one message read.

Mama's pager buzzed and her cell phone rang. She tried hard to ignore the messages, hiding her devices under car seat cushions and in the trunk. He kept paging and calling, telling her he'd gotten a good deal on one of the fighting cocks.

"Did I mention there's water?" yet another message on her pager insisted.

"Make it stop! It's giving me a headache! I can't breathe!" Mama said in the driver's seat.

"Just turn it off, Mama," I said, pressing down on the button.

"My head's going to explode. Every time it beeps, my head throbs."

"I turned it off. It's okay now. Your head won't explode."

"Good. I feel better. How's my hair?" She looked in the rearview mirror.

What Mama ignored consciously, she drank unknowingly: the constant mention of water running through pipes and streaming out of faucets. The messages kept coming. And before we knew it, she was pulling the van up to the driveway and parking it where the red carpet used to be—where I last saw Papa at the house. With one swing of the main doors, she opened the floodgates for provisions that had been withheld from us for years. Norman waited at the foyer, just a foot to the right of the gold console mirror, his arms outstretched for hers and his deep chest voice proclaiming, "Lights! Air-conditioning! A television! The real deal! And water. Did I mention we have running water?"

Mama quickly forgot about meals and refreshments offered by strangers and friends. There was a faucet waiting to fill a tumbler, a kettle ready to boil. She forgot about living in the van and dancing in the rain. Mama ran to her bathroom, and I ran to mine. She turned the gold knobs on the Jacuzzi, stripped off her clothes, and sat in the middle of the whirlpool. The jets hadn't been used in years, so the first spurt of water came out yellow brown. She bathed in it anyway.

Upstairs, I closed the bathroom door behind me and stepped into my indoor rainfall. We luxuriated in what should have been a normal part of our lives. As water rinsed off lather after lather, we let our baths wash away the manifestos we'd established the week before:

"That we will find a way out of the mansion!"

"That Norman is no boss to us!"

That she and I were a team.

We soaped and sang. All while Norman sat on his side of the bed in an unbuttoned white shirt and drank his whiskey, his aqua vitae, swirling the caramel-colored spirit in his wide-brimmed, thick-base old-fashioned glass. He swirled, sniffed the sweetness and strength, and then swigged.

Whiskey, neat, was how he liked it—not on the rocks, as we didn't have ice in the mansion for years. Whiskey, neat—no frills and no fuss, just straight up. The quicker it was ready, the sooner it was drunk. And the sooner it hit his brain.

After an hour-long wash, I turned the TV on in Paolo's old room. I flipped channels as I got dressed. Once I found *Wansapanataym*, Filipino adaptations of Disney tales, I lay on my stomach with my hair dripping wet and watched a brown-skinned Cinderella hop into her kalabasa carriage. The preteen that I was gushed and tee-heed at the on-screen romance between princess and prince. I was a normal kid again.

And then the scream.

It was the scream I had been waiting to hear since Norman stepped into the mansion, like a fire alarm I saw someone pull the day he barreled into our world. Someone had long ago broken the glass and pulled down the lever, but not until now had the alarm gone off. Mama was supposed to be the alarm but was missing parts or was short-circuited, and her reaction was several years delayed.

There was the call and I was the responder. I got up in one jump, reached my hand under the pillow, grabbed the fork I'd been hiding for four years, and ran downstairs with my weapon held in front of me, like a soldier with his rifle searching for an enemy. I thought of my friends forsaken in the killing fields of Abra: *bang-bang*.

Paolo and I had trained for this moment—the time when one of us was to kill the Common Enemy. We had practiced in our many play-times before: how to wield a makeshift weapon, how to load ammunition—pellets in a BB gun, how to throw a grenade of talcum powder, how to stay in hiding and remain silent for days or years, how to survive a drought or famine or a forty-day monsoon, how to ambush, and how to retrieve.

I now had to retrieve my mother.

The long dark hallway led me to the master bedroom, Norman's lair, where the door had been left a quarter of the way open—as though someone was trying to make an exit but was stopped in her tracks; as if someone was making an escape but had made the mistake of looking back and was abruptly, forcefully, prevented from leaving.

The scream went on and then transformed into heaving-sobbing-groaning. I walked closer, fork still held straight out in front of me at throat level. I kicked the door open and swung myself back against the hallway wall, like they did in Paolo's video games and Papa's favorite Steven Seagal cop dramas. I poked my head in, followed by my fork, and lastly, by my foot. I smelled the concoction of whiskey and blood in the air. I saw splats of almost-black red on the wall—bigger splats at midway, and smaller specks toward the ceiling. The splash of blood had come from head level and the blunt force from somewhere below. Mama was curled up on her side, writhing on the floor like a worm in a salt bath. She looked smaller than a child and no bigger than the pool of crimson circled around her.

I knelt down, touched her head with my free hand, and felt a mat of sticky hair—the long, shiny black hair she or the maids used to brush a hundred strokes a night. Now her hair was shiny not from cautious combing but from the fragments of glass lodged in the crown of her forgotten beauty.

Norman sat up on his side of the bed, his lower half under the satin duvet. He leaned against the velvet headboard with eyes glazed from rage and alcohol, his lower lip drooping, and his jaw juddering and covered in spit. His left hand held a bottle of whiskey while his right curled up in the shape of an invisible wide-brimmed, thick-base old-fashioned glass. He never turned his head to me, so I didn't know if he knew I was there. He looked straight ahead, examining his artwork on the wall: little dots and big dots of my mother's blood.

"I'm here to help you, Mama," I whispered as I put her arm around my neck.

"I'm sorry," she said, as tears mixed with blood in the corners of her eyes and the wrinkles around her lips.

"It's okay, Mama. We got to go. I got you."

Norman grunted.

"Come on, Mama. Get up. Come on."

Norman grunted again as he pulled off the satin duvet and uncovered his legs.

"Come on, Mama. Get up or we'll both be dead," I said as I hoisted her up with all my twelve-year-old, ninety-five-pound strength. I pulled her arms over my shoulders and around my neck, wearing her like a backpack, the fork still in my sweaty, bloody hand. Her breath felt warm on my neck, reminding me that she was, in fact, still alive.

I stumbled down the long dark hallway, the main steps, and the driveway, Mama breathing slower and slower, as I breathed faster and faster, panting and puffing with my every step. Her hair covered my hair, dampening it with the trickle from the crack on her crown. The blood covering my hands and her arms made us lose grip of each other several times. I re-clutched her arms and pulled her body up on my back again—the way Papa used to do when he'd piggyback me and I'd start slipping down. With every step, I told my body to keep on—heels and arches on and off the ground, legs advancing, pelvis and rib cage pressing away from Norman and toward the wrought-iron gates and the sinking sun. I nearly tripped over bundles of campaign T-shirts scattered on the floor. I stepped on chicken shit, lumps of turd caking on my bare soles.

After much struggle, I reached the end of the driveway, untangled the metal chain that held the gates closed, and slid the rusty, five-pound metal rod off the gate hook, one yank at a time. Moonlight and starlight led me to the side of the highway where I could hail a cab. None came. I prayed, "God, help us."

Still, there came no cabs, no jeepneys, no passersby. I prayed again, "God, help us."

A pedicab stopped. The young man got off the trike, *tsk-tsk*ing as he helped me get Mama on the plastic-wrapped, duct-taped seat. I recognized the young man—it was the boy who had given me, Elma, and our buckets of water a free ride from the pozo. He'd called me "Mam" and Elma "Maganda." And now he was pedaling us away from the mansion and to Santo Niño Hospital, where I had once lain unconscious after falling off a slide. Although the low-class, low-tech hospital was my mother's last choice for health care, it had saved me once before. And now it was to save me—and *her*—once again.

The pedicab boy parked his trike on the curb, carried Mama into the emergency room, and sat her between a bandaged man in grease-covered jeans and a laboring woman in a fraying dress. I wanted to give the pedicab boy something for his help, but I had nothing but a bloody fork. Before I could even thank him, he said, "It's nothing." Then he gave me a salute for a goodbye, turned around, and pedaled on.

I sat on the floor across the hall from Mama, about three meters away, leaning against the wall opposite from her. I crossed my arms in front of me, clutching the fork under my right arm. I watched Mama droop in her seat, be examined by a nurse, and then rolled off on a gurney to a curtained-off room. I watched through the part in the curtains how they wiped her clean of blood, shaved a patch of her hair, sewed her up, and bandaged her cracked head. I watched the doctors huddle around her, invite two cops into the room, and ask her what had happened.

I saw everything and heard everything, but could say nothing.

"I fell," Mama said. "I fell down the stairs with a glass in this hand. My head landed where the glass had shattered."

"Are you sure?" the cops asked a couple of times.

"Yes."

That was it. I got up, took three steps to the nearest trash can, and flung the fork in. We both could've died that night, and there she was, lying to those who could've helped us, those who could've found a way out. They could've found Papa or Paolo or my yaya. They could've even taken us to the precinct, let us sleep on a cot on the floor, and kept us away from Norman. But no. Mama asked to be escorted home, to be driven in a clunky cop car back to the mansion.

One of Norman's crooks stood in front of the wrought-iron gates, waiting for our return home—as if he and his boss were sure that we'd be back that night. He walked Mama up the driveway and the main steps, then down the long dark hallway, and toward the master bedroom. I trailed behind them without making a sound, exhausted from sprinting my mother to momentary safety. Norman came out of the room, more sober than drunk, but drunk nonetheless. They locked eyes and stood there, as though nobody else shared the space and air with them.

He held a glass filled with something clear and offered it to Mama and said while brushing the hair off her face, "I'm sorry, honey. I didn't mean to hurt you. You know I didn't mean to. Here's some water."

Mama, sniffling and hurting, reached her hand forward and took the glass.

I ran upstairs, stomping hard on the floor, knowing exactly what Mama was doing below: she was lying next to Norman and was, sip by sip and drop by drop, drinking the water.

No Fisher of Men

Papa never made it to the desert, so he gave the ocean a try.

His daughter from his first marriage, Lucia, had started a family with Danilo, a pharmaceutical representative. Together, they built a catering company and shared an office with Papa's first son, Luis, a cargo-delivery servicer. The office sat adjacent to the Entrepreneurial Union of the Philippines, a nongovernmental organization that granted funds to entrepreneurial socioeconomic and environmental projects.

During a visit with his first family, Papa came across the cooperative and quickly forged a friendship with them. His visionary way of life, his personal messianic purpose, his flight toward the sun, had finally found a group of social scientists that could help realize his dream of saving the world while making a living.

Fishermen trying to provide for their families and keep up with the national and international appetite for seafood had adopted a dangerous way of catching fish. At the time, dynamite fishing had become a necessary evil in the Philippine Islands. The use of dynamite initially proved to be profitable, but it soon depleted coastal towns of healthy fish habitat. The explosives flattened coral reefs and killed marine animals and fish eggs. It sometimes killed fishermen, too. The daily catch steadily dropped below subsistence needs. Inland ecosystems failed and forced fishermen to venture farther out to sea. Boating to the deep Pacific reduced their time for supplemental crop farming. Deep-sea fishing also increased the risk of their getting caught in a storm, running across pirates, and falling prey to creatures too large and too ferocious, or yet unnamed.

But Papa found a way to save them. He traveled to Tokyo and the Niigata Prefecture to study Japanese net technology. From there he learned a new way about stationary large-net fishing: a system that used three large nets suspended from buoys. The Japanese used the first net as a decoy—it hung from the surface to the seafloor like a straight-line curtain, blocking fish swimming against the current. On either ends of the straight-line floated basket nets the size of a tugboat, trapping fish that had tried to swim away from the first curtain of mesh. From these two baskets, a mechanical dipper scooped out the catch—the equivalent of the traditional Filipino fishing boat's three-week yield. With this system, bycatch such as dolphins, sharks, and sea turtles could be released. The system—which Papa developed, enhanced, and later named as Orionet— convinced the cooperative that it could save the industry, the towns-people, the environment, and Papa's last tad of vision and self-esteem.

Papa took jeepneys and trikes to coastal provinces such as Minas and Aticlan, rallying together and educating fishermen on how to adopt a new way of making a living, of prospering while caring for the earth. He convinced them that if they were to stop using dynamite and instead respected the waters, the ocean would then repay them with yield upon yield. The men, as the men on the sierra and in the desert had once done, trusted him with their trade and their lives. Papa, who was once Leo in the forest and Orion in Arabia, had become—at the dawn of the new millennium—the fisher of men.

The problem with great ideas was this: they could be stolen. People within local trade found out about Papa's plans. They rewarded townspeople and councilmen for tips on Papa's 2.0 technology. They pirated his principles and produced crude versions of the straight-line and basket nets. Papa operated on a small cooperative grant and could not keep up with their speed and yield. What he designed for one million pesos, they fabricated and distributed for less than a hundred thousand. Their operations destroyed Papa's last undertaking and squeezed him of his last cent.

The ocean lured other industrialists to the salt and sand of Minas and Aticlan, and diverted Papa away from a new moneymaking, man-saving deal. It blew him far from the tides and back to the metro. Without saying goodbye to his new friends, Papa turned his back to the sea. He remembered that he had always been afraid of the deep blue, of drowning. Papa had never learned to swim. And he was sinking now. He decided to go back inland to find his family—to find me.

Millennium

We were two months out of hurricane season. At general assembly, instead of singing another patriotic song or listening to an alumnus speak, we sat our bottoms on the cold gymnasium floor through two or so hours of a lecture on how to live without contact with the outside world, without electric power, without running water, without food, without light, and possibly, if things were not to be resolved soon after midnight of December 31, how to live without certainty or security or an ounce of feeling good.

"Wind your watches often and make sure you move your wrists," the demonstrator said, turning the knob on her watch. "Your pulses keep the watches from stopping."

The girls sitting next to me wound their watches. Everyone at school had made the rather unusual switch from digital to analog—from Casio Baby-G water-resistant watches to hand-wound, no-battery, Swiss-made timepieces. I sat back as they all hunched forward, manipulating their tickers and studying the mechanics of pre-digital design.

The principal took the stage. She warned against food shortages, electricity blackouts, and scheduled water rations. My classmates believed her. They murmured to each other and gestured with their hands: "What in the world?! What will we do?"

I smirked in my seat as they busied themselves with foolproofing against the doom that was to come.

Later that day, our science teacher had us watch a VHS movie called *Y2K Family Survival Guide*. The documentary encouraged using the stairs and avoiding air travel on the last week of the year. The narrator warned about billions of wires, computer chips, and codes self-destructing at the turn of the century. I watched my classmates and teacher take fright and become overwrought. They stared at the television screen almost without blinking and in a daze of dread. I had read from an old issue of *Time* that belonged to the library that the media cycle was two weeks long. That meant that every two weeks, the television people and the newspaper people and the magazine people got to decide what would occupy our minds: hope or fear.

The film bored me. Nothing about it alarmed me because I had been living through what it foreshadowed. Although I had my own panic, my own survival to plan, I could not help but hide my face in my hands—and laugh.

The film went on. It recommended installing generators and stocking up on bottled water, canned goods, matchsticks, candles, and mosquito coils. It referenced the use of Doberman guard dogs against looters and suggested special authentication procedures against swindlers. My classmates agonized over the possibility of hell on earth. They bit their nails and jittered before the apocalyptic images flashing on the screen.

Ticktock. Suddenly, the world had to get prepared to scrounge, scour, collect, keep safe, keep momentum, and stay alive. At the end of 1999, the world and I finally became in sync—and all because of zeros in a computer chip.

We were running, running, running out of time.

The only parts left unaffected by the scare were the convent next door and the mansion. The nuns had long ago taken a vow of silence, of simplicity, and of poverty, and so technology never became their way of life. And we in the mansion had long ago lost all things worldly, all things material, and all things normal. Norman had stopped paying the water and electric bills once again. And so the threat of losing something, or everything, did not frighten us one bit. If anything, Mama and Norman took advantage of the hysteria and the peril predicted to come. They preyed on the paranoid.

"Estrella!" Norman hollered as he walked up the main steps. "Call a meeting with the sheriff! I got a plan!"

I snooped from behind the lanai door.

Mama met him by the console mirror and said, "Tell me."

"We use the leftover silk-screen paint to make Y2K shirts. We sell them on the street, *boom!* Easy money."

"I like it," Mama said, her head still bandaged.

"And we use the old press to make more deeds. Everyone will be panic buying. Why not sell them property, you know?"

They walked to the breakfast room and ordered Tony to bring merienda. I ran upstairs, worried that they would, yet again, entangle me in their business plans and propaganda. I went into my room and sat on the edge of my bed, thinking that fighting the Common Enemy was no longer enough. I needed a greater motivation: a destination and not merely a place from which to depart. I took a notebook out of my backpack and made a list of things to find: a normal home, a family, and the ocean.

I was not simply leaving the mansion. I was going somewhere.

At school the next day, the waiting area smelled just like afternoon: sweat, cut grass, fumes from cars driving by, and the aftermath of a three o'clock sun-shower. High school girls stole minutes with suitors, pressing their faces between bars for kisses and receiving bouquets. Younger students checked their wristwatches as they waited for their rides home. The air buzzed with teen gossip and cars honked to summon passengers. The noise was familiar. But then a swarming sound traveled from down the road and toward the school gate: a disharmony, a cacophony of teen boy trouble. The whole waiting room turned toward the direction of disturbance and found a throng of students from an all-boys school with batons and bats. The boys rushed toward the group of suitors stealing kisses and passing flowers, and in a unified motion clobbered the infatuation out of their pubescent bodies.

A heavyset boy took a lanky one by the shirt and slammed him repeatedly against the metal gate. The girls in the waiting room stepped back with every *pang!* A group of five circled around a boy who was still holding on to his bouquet of gerberas. They kicked him and he recoiled. The boys blasted at one another until the security guards came, whistle-blowing and handcuffing, and sorting the group between hospital- and jail-bound. And as the fight quelled and we in the waiting room sidled back toward the gate, I found him—manacled to gate bars and bleeding from one eyebrow.

"Kuya?"

He looked up.

"Kuya, what are you doing here?"

"I'm happy to see you," he said, choking up and realizing that his delinquency had brought him back to me. "I wasn't sure if you were still at this school, you know, or if Mama had pulled you out."

"I'm happy to see you, too," I said, looking him up and down, and recognizing the tone of his skin, the way he left one side of his shirt untucked, and his well-defined thumbs calloused from playing video games. "Why are you so skinny?"

"Why are *you* so skinny?" he said.

"You know why," I whispered so that nobody else could hear.

"Mama told me things were better at home. She said she was taking good care of you and that she could afford to feed you, but not me."

I shook my head. "We don't have food, water, electricity. Lots of bad people and strange people come in and out of the house."

"Why didn't you tell me?" he said as he gestured *why* with his cuffed hands.

"How?"

People stared at us, like they were finding out our secret. The room stopped and our onlookers watched. They filled the air with whispers, with speculations. The brawl was no longer the afternoon's big event.

"I'm sorry." He started to whimper, wiping his tears on his bloodied sleeve.

"It's not your fault, Kuya."

"A long time ago, I gave you my Game Boy. I promised to take care of you."

"It's okay, Kuya."

"It's not. I will get you out."

The guards came and unshackled him from the gate. They dragged him to a cop car, and right before they shut the door, Paolo stuck his head out to inform me that he got a soccer scholarship from the university and a night job as a DJ.

"They're paying for me to play soccer and music! It's my way out! I will get you out, too!" he said.

I stuck my arm through the gate and waved, standing at the far end of the waiting room, sniffling and blubbering under my breath. My brother was leaving his boyhood and entering a new life, and he was to keep his promise of ushering me into mine.

He will get me out. I know it.

I killed time at the library the last weeks before Christmas break. I did very little reading, as the librarians had grown chatty the week before the bug was supposed to obliterate all. The stocking-wearing women who manned the circulation desk spoke more words at the end of 1999 than they did during my first eight years at the private school. The one who had introduced me to J. D. Salinger became particularly verbose— she cajoled me every afternoon into signing up for the interscholastic writing contest.

"That history teacher of yours, Santiago, sees talent in you. He's spoken of it before," the librarian said. "You should have him coach you for the competition. I'll vouch for you—I know which books you frequently check out. I know you're well-read. I *know*."

I found a sign-up form in my cubby the next day. Paper-clipped to it was a note from Mr. Santiago, telling me to fill out the sheet and to read up on current events—the contest was to focus on new millennium issues. Later that day, I asked the librarian for the paper, which, again, she loaned me "indefinitely."

"Win that prize money," she said.

I thought about what I could do with the cash: jeepney fare, a bus ticket, books, coins to telephone Papa with, an investment in Elma's sari-sari.

That night, I studied the red-and-black pages slipped into my backpack by my fairy bookmother. I read them under candle- and coil-light, praying, "God, forgive me if this is stealing. I need the papers to win the contest. Please help me."

Every morning a new note appeared in my cubby and with it came a magazine clipping or a photocopy of a book chapter. Each one was about a topic that was already familiar to me: separation of the classes, the Gulf War, natural disasters, political rivalries, childhood hunger, and warfare. I read up. I circled words I didn't know: *ramification, stratification, dysentery.* I thought of Mama calling out words to the morning air, expanding our vocabulary while hurling hollowware. I wished that I could ask her to define the words for me, that I could sit next to her in bed or on the armrest of her peacock chair and ask her what the words meant.

The night before the competition, I arranged in my backpack a bouquet of pencils from my friend Bunny and a legal pad the librarian had also indefinitely loaned me. Instead of stuffing my backpack with crumpled paper and Coke bottles, I stashed in it a fat ream of reading material. Before bed, I used an extra centimeter of water for my sponge bath, combed my hair a hundred strokes like my yaya used to do, and slipped under my crunchy, moth-eaten sheets for an early turn-in and a good night's rest.

The next morning, I got in the Land Cruiser with Norman and Mama, thinking that they hadn't suspected my mission for the day. I was right. They knew nothing about the writing contest that Mr. Santiago had signed me up for. They detoured from our usual route to school to the opposite side of the metro.

"Wait! Where are we going?" I said, sitting in the cargo space.

"You're missing school today for a special project," Mama said.

"No! I don't want to be part of any of your projects! Take me to school! I *have* to be at school today!" I said as I slipped my arms through my backpack's straps and grabbed on to the door handle, forcing open the child-locked hatchback door.

"Hey!" Norman yelled. "You're gonna break the fuckin' door! Sit down and calm down! We're taking you to a fuckin' job interview—a tryout. Isn't this what you've always wanted to do? *Write?* You're always bringing home books and doodling in your fuckin' notebooks!"

"I have to be at school! I have something important at school!"

"What's more important than this? I'm finally letting you do something you want to do! The *Philippine Inquirer* is hiring junior writers— your chance to do what you love and make me some money," Mama said, brushing the hair off my face.

"I'm not making you any money!" I said as I yanked the door handle up and down. "Take me back to school!"

"Calm down and shut up. We're already here," Mama said as the Land Cruiser slowed to a stop.

Tony pulled me out of the cargo space and dragged me into the *Philippine Inquirer* building. Norman remained in the car, and Mama tromped up to the front desk. I breathed hard through my teeth and through the hair on my face as Mama wrote my name on the form fastened to a clipboard. She sat me on a chair in the queue, wiped the hair off my face one more time, forced the clipboard between my chest and crossed arms, and said, "We'll be back when it's over. Make me proud and make me some money."

I wanted to spit at her face but resolved to take my revenge on paper. I waited for someone to call my name, and as soon as they did, I marched my way to a seat in a room full of aspiring writers, all under the age of sixteen, and wrote away. I wrote so hard into the paper that I punctured it at every punctuation and vowel. The contest proctor told us to write a review of a book or a film, and although I could have written about Holden Caulfield, I instead wrote *like* Holden Caulfield. I plowed my pen through each line, scattering curse words on the page like the chicken shit spattered all over our house.

I wrote about the three things I knew well: architecture, landscape, and weather—my childhood. Each represented my mother.

I divided my essay into three sections. The first section began, "My mother is the mansion." She was a labyrinthine edifice with gold-plated doorknobs and marble floors, but with no water and no food. She was the house with too many rooms because she had too many secrets to keep, too many versions of herself to shelter: the mother who'd lost children to prematurity and drugs, the princess who so badly wanted to be queen, the con artist who sold fake deeds, the guerilla girl with red politics and red nails. She, like the mansion, rose three stories high to the heavens and sank deep into the ground. The basement closet—her innermost part.

Then, "My mother is this land." Unruly, untamable, an archipelago—a country made up of floating islands, born of lava, a republic tended to by servants and farmers. She, like the land, boasted troughs and peaks, quaked, avalanched. But she, too, smelled like orchid, like orange peel, like rain drying on cement.

And lastly, on that note, "My mother is the monsoon." She fell and took everything down with her. Like cloudburst, she spun around the city, hovered, found a target, then blasted to drown us. She, Little Benny, was meant to be the star—but when she came falling, she forgot that she was supposed to twinkle. Instead, she shot down to us as a storm. When Tachio died, I saw her wail. She rained tears. She became her tears: cold, incessant.

Deluge. Delusional.

Breaking into a million pieces.

I was drowning in a monsoon of her.

The timer buzzed. I got up from my seat, stomped to the front of the room, and flung the clipboard across the proctor's desk. I scrunched the essay into my skirt pocket and marched out of the room and through the building's doors. The Land Cruiser pulled up as if on cue, and I jumped into the cargo space.

Mama asked, "So how'd it go?"

And I said, "Very well. I wrote what I had to."

On Nochebuena, every house but ours twinkled with Christmas lights and capiz shell parol. Our house was the largest but quietest on the highway. While families feasted on lechón, hamonado, and fruit salad in condensed milk, I fed myself gelatinous blood cake and mashed mungo bean. I overheard the singing from my window and caroled along, singing of Jesus's heavenly birth.

I sang with them softly, purring as I watched the tiny bulbs of green, red, and white glitter outside. Softer and softer, I sang. And as my voice became muted, the sound of someone's steps became more audible.

"You're leaving!" Elma said as she swung my door open.

"What? When?"

"You're leaving tonight," she so casually said. She pronounced the words without stutter, without sentiment, without pause, without dread.

I hugged her and she squeezed me back. Then she shrugged me off and said, "You have to pack. Dali!"

I packed clothes, books, and pictures—one of me with Papa and Paolo by a waterfall, one of me and Paolo cuddling in a crib, one of me with Mama, who in the photo was plump and pregnant with Tachio, and lastly, me under a chandelier—its crystals giving luster to objects below.

Elma zipped the duffel bag, grabbed my hand, and ran me out of the room. She pulled me away from the upstairs bedrooms, down the steps, past the cathedral window, through the long dark hallway, and to the main doors. "Sige! Halika na!"

Mama, who must have been cleaning her scalp wounds or powdering her face, heard the scurry of our steps. She tottered around the bed that Norman drunk-dozed in and charged to where we were—only to be stopped by Elma, the dormant volcano whose boil was inside.

She erupted at my mother. "You cannot stop her! You will have to skin me alive before you keep her from leaving this damned house! You and I will die in this mansion together, but not my friend. She will leave tonight." Then she uttered Mama's favorite word, "Puñeta!"

Mama gasped. She opened her palm and swung it back behind her. But instead of slapping Elma, she cupped her hand over her mouth and fell to the floor. She wailed the same wail she let out the night my baby brother died, the night I first feared her.

Elma turned back around to my direction and opened the main doors. In the shaft of moonlight coming through, she embraced me one last time while weeping and said, "Your books and pictures will remind you of everything: heartaches, lessons, joys. Find the ocean. Write."

"I'm sorry, Elma," I said, holding her tight with eyes closed, as if to squeeze her spirit out of the dark skin that encased it—out of the life that entrapped her.

"Nothing is your fault. Now go."

I let go of her and I let go of life in the mansion.

Amen.

I placed the crumpled letter I'd written to Mama on the console under the mirror and ran down the main steps—time *tick-tock*ing to the hour of the birth of our dear Lord—and toward the garden where my dead baby brother slept almost two meters under. I knelt down and patted the now-grassless earth and said, "I love you."

I stood back up and ran down the driveway and to the wrought-iron gates. I untangled the metal chain that held the gates closed. Moonlight and starlight led me to the side of the highway, where my other friend, the pedicab boy, waited. He took the duffel bag and escorted me to the cellophane-wrapped seat, where I sat as he pedaled away and away, to clear skies and toward the direction of the pozo. With his left foot's every step on the pedal, I inhaled. And with his right foot's every crank on the magical machine, I breathed out and healed.

We reached the well where I first met Diyosa, and where I had many times fetched water with Elma, and there we found a Mitsubishi L300 van that was reconfigured to look like a jeepney. A woman in her thirties stepped out of the vehicle and reached her hand to me and said, "Do you remember me, Neng? I am your sister, Lucia." She took the duffel bag from my hand and brushed the hair off my face. She kissed me on the cheek and told me that Paolo had found Papa, and Papa had found her, but that Papa felt undeserving of my custody.

"Our father will always be chasing after opportunity," she said. "But I have made a home with my husband and three kids, and we live next door to our brother, Luis, and his family. We will be your home now."

Papa had always told me that we were not meant for normal, and for that, he was sorry. But at the end of the millennium, he finally accepted that although we had our eccentricities, what might have been best all along was a normal childhood, a normal family, a normal home—mercy in the mundane.

Lucia opened the door to the back of the van, slowly and delightedly, as if unwrapping for me my first Christmas present in ten years. I peered in and saw, dangling from bar handles, tumbling across seats, and poking at each other, toddlers and preschoolers and preteens: my new tribe.

They filled the van with giggling and the smell of shampoo. They were bathed and their clothes were clean and without holes. Lucia stood next to me and held the van door open. Her blouse felt soft against my elbow.

The man in the driver's seat, Lucia's husband, turned up the radio's volume and said, "You like music? I have lots of mixed CDs. Here, pick one."

He passed a book with transparent sleeves holding discs. One of the boys, wide-eyed and just learning to speak, crunched on a prawn cracker as he toddled to me with the discs. He handed me the book and offered me a bite of his snack.

The only girl in the group of children, about eight years old, brushed my hair with her fingers, and said, "Pretty."

Lucia wrapped an arm around me as she sat me next to her in the van. She asked, "What's your Christmas wish?"

I didn't have to think. I had prayed for this moment many times.

"Can you take me to the ocean?"

"Christmas by the sea? Sounds like a good plan. Tell me, though, why there?" my sister asked me.

She would ask me this question at several other occasions between seventh grade and my college graduation: when I signed up to play soccer in Gothenburg, Sweden, when I saved my allowance to visit the largest bookstore in Hong Kong, when she moved to the suburbs, and I to the city, and when I transplanted to the South with my college boyfriend to start a handmade business, get a master of fine arts, and start a family by the sea. I looked at my sister and said, "Because I've never been a runner, but I sure can swim." I was not simply leaving the mansion. I was going somewhere.

The Season of the Sun

The sun has one kind of splendor,
the moon another
and the stars another;
and star differs from star in splendor.

—1 Corinthians 15:41

2016

I am married now and live close to the ocean.

The man whom I call my husband is kind, patient, loving, generous, and gentle, much like my father. But he lacks Papa's desire to save the world. Instead, this man devotes himself to the daily building and rebuilding of mine: my world as his passion. He works from eight in the morning to nine at night, dividing his time between being a private school teacher, a college instructor, and a candlemaker. He works this hard and this much so I can spend my days at my home studio, writing, sketching, and dreaming up things.

He introduced himself to me at a rooftop event on the corner of Sixth Avenue and Thirty-Seventh Street. It was June 2006, my first summer as a college student in New York City.

He said, "I want to be your friend forever."

Only Elma had ever pledged such a declaration, a commitment, to me and because of the life I had lived and the evil I had seen, I'd been wary of anyone who'd tried to get close. I had made myself as interesting as possible—fashionable, literary, artistic, musical—so that both strangers and friends would become so caught up with my present that they would be uninterested in my past. But in him, I sensed Elma's spirit: able to bend and sway, able to wait, able to laugh through hardship, and whose boil inside explodes to—and only to—protect me.

"Tell me everything," he said, in his rolled-up khakis and slim-fit, sky-blue oxford shirt.

Over a shared Wendy's Frosty or a rice bowl from a hole-in-the-wall at St. Mark's Place, I recounted my childhood in the big, bad, bloody, beautiful mansion. I told him, most times through tears, about the forts I had built with my brother, bedtime tales my father shared, my mother's basement closet and parties, the ladies of the evening, Norman's goons and guns, my pets, the chickens, the pozo, Diyosa, and Elma.

"You two are so alike," I said. "Funny how you were born to different families, different worlds, and yet have the same heart and spirit. It's like my old friend is right here with me."

He went back to South Carolina at the end of the summer. We kept in touch, in love, through email, text messages, letters, and phone calls. Once he had unlocked the metal gates to my past—one *uunnkk-uunnkk* at a time—little could be done to stop the flood, the monsoon, and its relentlessness.

"I am breaking," I said.

"You're becoming a new kind of beautiful," he replied.

He sent me CDs: compilations of hip-hop, R&B, pop, and indie tunes he liked. "Listen to these when you get scared or sad." Just like my brother, he believed in the healing power of music, in how a rhythm or a lyric can redeem a day.

He asked me what I wanted to do with my life.

And I said, "I want to write."

"Then go write. Write it all," he said.

By encouraging me to put pen to paper, he walked me back to and through the past and into a new time: the season of the sun.

We dated long-distance for three years until I followed him to the South, to pink-and-orange Carolina skies, to water. And from there, we started a family. We flew back to New York on Labor Day weekend for a fifty-person wedding at Central Park, where we vowed our love and loyalty to God, to each other, to the arts, to academia, and to becoming a well of love, light, and kindness to those around us.

I married him and gave him stories. He married me and gave me two things: a mother and a daughter.

His mother's name is Mary, like Mara, the sister I never met. But also like Mary, the mother of Jesus, the unassuming virgin, the nurturer. Our Lady of Peace and Voyage. She sends gift cards for coffee and gas; stocks our pantry with peanut butter, crackers, noodles, and grits; shares my affinity for local honey and homemade soap; checks up on our dog and our succulents; and takes me out to lunch so she can listen to my stories.

"Had I been there, honey, I would've held you," she says every time. "I am so proud of all that you've done and all that you have yet to do."

She introduces me to neighbors and coworkers as "not my daughter-in-law, but my daughter." She links arms with me and rubs my upper arm when we walk through Belk department store, asking, in her midland dairy-farm accent, "You okay, honey?"

She, too, has endured hardship, the quiet southern gothic kind, and so can sense when the tremble in my voice comes from something other than strong coffee. On my birthday and on holidays, when I think of Mama, Papa, Paolo, and Tachio the most, she sends cards with cash folded in, *for a most beautiful outfit for the most beautiful daughter,* or an owl-shaped soap, or a bag of granola and a magazine clipping with a note penciled, *Read this. Made me think of you. I hope writing is going well.*

Mary was there, the only one permitted by us to come, at the birth of our daughter. Mary stroked the hair off my face as I moaned in pain and pushed in the birthing pool. I chose to deliver this way because I was, still am, most comfortable in and around water. Anika Louise was born the week of Thanksgiving 2011, into a ninety-six-degree aqueous environment. I scooped her out of the pool and to my chest, whispering, "My baby, my sunshine."

She nuzzled into my bosom and suckled to feed without any coaching or coaxing from me or the delivery staff. She knew her way to my breasts, her sustenance, and knew her place in my arms. My husband cut the cord and Mary washed the baby. The first and last time I had seen an infant so fragile, lips still puckered, and flesh still wet and fresh from the sac was the night of my third birthday—Tachio's coming and going. But this baby, whom I had carried for thirty-six weeks and four days and had labored to meet for over forty hours, was plump like a mango and, like the fruit, bursting with brightness, sweetness, and color.

We christened her with her two names because of what they mean: Anika, Hebrew for grace. And Louise, a variation of Louis, which means strong warrior.

Grace and strength. Blessed warrior child.

She is almost six now. And I am teaching her how to read by having her sound out letters from Pablo Neruda's *Love Poems* and E. B. White's *Here Is New York.* Like my mother, I call out words to the air. It is how we teach our daughters to love language.

"Sonnet!"

"Periwinkle!"

"Kaleidoscope!"

"Beauty!"

"Charity!"

"Hope!"

On Fridays, my girl's day off from Montessori school, she stays home with me and we play music from our vinyl collection. I tell her, particularly when it's a Snoop Dogg or a TLC twelve-inch spinning, that my brother loved music. He still does.

"He's been working as a DJ since he was seventeen years old," I say. "He used to sneak up to the DJ booth at our mother's parties."

"Will he ever come to one of our dance parties?" she says, referring to mornings or evenings when we turn the volume all the way up on the Jensen Three-Speed and dance in our robes, pajamas, and homemade Mardi Gras masks.

"I hope so. He lives in Manila, which is halfway across the world."

"Tell me again about Manila."

And I tell her about Manila: the jeepneys, the highways, the street vendors, the tall buildings and large houses bordered by shanties and shacks, the sunsets, the women, the beggars, the old buildings and churches, the stray mammals on the side of the road, the birds hovering over rivers and paddies, and lastly, though I hesitate, the mansion.

"Tell me again about the princesses!" she says.

"My mama threw the most spectacular parties. The princesses—debutantes—wore ball gowns as wide as our coffee table. They danced under a puzzle of mirrors."

"The kaleidoscope!"

"Yes, my kaleidoscope."

"Now tell me again about the van!" she says, lying on her stomach and drawing hearts and writing *I love Mom* on an early draft of my manuscript.

I tell her about the van. I go into detail about joyrides, barkers, passengers, and mixtapes. And I narrate stories about escaping the mansion with my mother and living in the van for a string of nights.

"Were you scared?" she asks, like I used to ask my papa.

"Yeah, but your lolo always told me to be brave."

Papa followed me to the States two years after I arrived there, but he has yet to follow me to pink-and-orange skies. We talk on the phone two or three times a week, and he tells me, in the same diplomatic, charismatic, and heroic voice he's always spoken in, that he needs the hustle of the city to keep him alive. *If I die, they die.*

"I'm brave, too," my girl says, as she puts on the Super Rainbow mask, cape, and belt I made for her. She climbs up onto the coffee table and assumes flight pose. "Super Rainbow!"

I tackle her to the rug and tickle her until she squeals, "No tickles!"

"No mercy!" I say. I grab her foot and run the tips of my fingers back and forth on her sole. "Little soldier, tell me all you know and I shall release you!"

"Never!" she says, gasping for breath.

I now have her locked down. I blow raspberries on her belly, and she gives in.

"The Beanie Boos sent me and they are hiding under the dining table!"

I pull her into me, just like I did the moment she was born, and forty pounds of her melt into the cradle of my arms. She stays there and tells me all her ideas: sea turtle rescues, volunteering at the South Carolina Aquarium, repurposing old crayons, the war against plastic bags, building scooters for three-legged cats, and selling pink lemonade, purple lemonade, and lime-green lemonade.

The record stops spinning and she gets up. "I can do it, Mama."

So independent, so me. *Strong will, this one. I like it.*

She lifts the dust cover, places the Peter Pan soundtrack on the platter, and positions the tonearm and needle on the record's perimeter. The record spins and she twirls. The hem of her sleeping shirt parachutes up. She hops up once again onto the coffee table, curls her index finger into a hook, and sings in her pirate voice. "Sing, Mama, sing!"

"Hold on," I say as I scuffle to my closet. I come back out to the living room in the Tiger Lily costume I made for Halloween two years back. I say, "Not so fast, Captain Hook!" and I aim my invisible arrow at her invisible ship. She grabs a handful of confetti—we always have colorful paper shreds all around the house—and she scrunches them into a ball in her hands. She launches and says, "C'mon, Lost Boys! Cannonball!"

One . . . two . . . three . . . BOOM!

We look at the mess between us—the mess we have made together—and laugh.

We are both back on the floor, making snow angels in the confetti, and rolling from side to side to tempt Skye, our seven-pound Maltese dog, to pounce on us and nibble on our collars and sleeves. Anika Louise tells me she is hungry as she shields her face from doggie kisses. So I walk to the kitchen to make grits and fish—food for my half-southern, half-Filipino, full-of-ideas, brown-skinned, black-haired, her-own-kind-of-warrior girl.

Over lunch, she says to the dog, "We need to be thankful for food because Mama didn't have food when she was little."

She gives him a bite of her bounty. Then she asks, "Mama, do you miss your mama?"

"I do, but it's better to miss her than to be around her."

"Because she does things that hurt people?"

That's how I've explained it to her: that my mother cannot come near us because she does regrettable things.

When I told Mama I was getting married: "A backyard wedding?! How cheap!"

When she received news about my pregnancy: "Well, you'll get fat!"

When I told her I decided to breastfeed: "Your breasts will sag!"

When I told her we were buying our first home: "You don't want a home. Send me your savings instead."

When I told her I was writing a book: "Well, it better make me some money because I taught you how to read and write. You get your smarts from me. You owe me everything."

My answer to Mama's declarations and direction: *I pledge to never become you.*

Never.

I tell Anika Louise that my mother is like the mansion: once opulent, strong, and handsome but crumbled over time. *Her weeping was the mansion's very voice.*

And Anika Louise, although young, knows to change the subject when necessary. Like Mary, she senses the shift in my tone or manner when I begin to get sad about my parents, my siblings, or the mansion.

This is when she asks, "Can we go to the pool?"

I say yes because the answer to this question is always yes.

It is the season of the sun.

We arrive at the neighborhood pool at a time when nobody is there. All the neighbors are at work and their children attend school full-time. We have the figure-eight-shaped pool all to ourselves. We peel down and jump in.

And she tells me, "I think today is the day."

And I know exactly what she means. She means that because her daddy and I allow her room to self-lead, when she gives the cue, we follow. And these are today's cues: goggles over eyes, hands on waist, and feet straddled to hip width. "Watch me, Mama!" She brings her arms overhead and rockets off the steps.

"I'm watching, my sunshine!"

She swims toward me, and I am breathing in her courage, for her courage is my joy. She swims, stroking away the water between us with her butterfly arms. She tips her chin up once for air and gulps. She drinks in oxygen and looks up at the sky. I am watching, watching, waiting. She can see my legs underwater and I can see her form from up top. Her figure is a diamond in the water—two points—diver hands and mermaid tail. And she is shining, sparkling, gliding underneath the hot sun.

I receive her with open arms. I pull her out of the water and into me. Exhausted from her lap, she lays her head on my shoulder. I wrap us in a floral towel and walk us to the cabana, and I sing to her.

I sing her my song of gray skies going, of promise and prayer. I sing to her, for she'll never know just how much I love her.

My girl, my sweetness.

The diamond in my palm.

Of stars, of sun.

She has touched the dark waters ebbing from my past.

With light. *Of light.*

ACKNOWLEDGMENTS

I thank God for surrounding me with such loving, caring, generous people:

My agent, Noah Ballard, whose faith in my work and story propelled me through the laborious writing and publishing of this book. He is a smart, meticulous, and devoted "agent who edits," and a friend to lean on during times of doubt and struggle. A superstar.

My editor at Little A, Vivian Lee, for her vision, encouragement, and precision. I wished for an editor who could appreciate the mayhem and magic of my childhood and understand the politics of being a female immigrant—and I got exactly what I wanted and needed. She was quick to compliment, but just as quick to demand that I flex my writing muscle—the perfect coach for what felt like a marathon for my heart and brain.

The team (made up of many teams) at Little A that has given this book so much care, so much thought, so much trust. I am thankful to be working with a publishing imprint that celebrates women, writers of color, immigrants, artists, and all sorts of hybrid identities and writing styles.

Mentors and teachers from my undergraduate, graduate, and writing-intensive programs: Catherine Oriani, Vicki Moss, Harry Bruinius, Lauren Rule Maxwell, Rick Mulkey, Susan Tekulve, Jim Minick, Dan

Wakefield, Richard Tillinghast, Bob Olmstead, Denise Duhamel, Leslie Pietrzyk, Suzanne Cleary, Marlin Barton, Ava Chin, Hua Hsu, M. Evelina Galang, and Elmaz Abinader. You have shepherded my voice and story into something that I thought could only happen in dreams. Thank you for giving of yourselves.

Workshop sisters and brothers: the creative nonfiction group ("the love mafia") at Converse College, local writers in Charleston, my students and clients, and my tribes at Kundiman and VONA/Voices. Two things we all know are true: creating is a communal act and writing can be lonesome. You carved a safe and joyful place for me to learn my craft and tell my story. You are C. S. Lewis's definition of friendship: *What! You, too?* Yes, me, too.

Friends—they know who they are—who made the process of writing and healing possible: giving rides, offering child care, listening and praying, attending a reading, donating to my Kickstarter, donating airline miles, asking the right questions, lending wisdom and courage and insight, referring me to a counselor, buying me bottles of wine, buying my family groceries, sending texts and emails and handwritten messages, watching me happy-cry or ugly-cry, and reminding me who I am and to whom I belong. You are the true champions.

My extended family in the Philippines, the United States (my mother-in-law and Aunt Franca, especially), and elsewhere who supported me through my education, early adulthood, and new motherhood. It takes great patience and faith to raise someone like me, and I owe an extraordinary debt to your grace and kindness.

My siblings, who each played a parental role when they should've been enjoying their growing-up years or their own children. My brothers and sister provided me with all that I lacked as a child: food, shelter, safety, and family. I somehow got them to answer questions and recall painful details to help me write this book. It was not easy, but we all learned from the process and were restored by it.

My parents, who love me in their unique ways. I owe my creativity, resilience, resourcefulness, and passion to them both—the very traits that make me a writer. My mother was brilliant and my father was ambitious, and I channeled much of their personas through the completion of this book. And I hope that I channeled their energies into something peaceful and life-giving. *Dona nobis pacem.*

My dog, Skye, who sat on my lap every day as I typed away.

My darling girl, who had just begun to walk when I first went on this wild writing ride. She is now almost six years old, is all about rainbows, curious, imaginative, thoughtful, and kind—the little light I needed through the diving back into darker times. She is my sunshine.

And last on this list but always first in my spirit, heart, and mind: my husband. We were twenty when he first asked me what I wanted to do with my life, when I told him about the mansion, when he encouraged me to transfer out of fashion school and into a writing program. We are in our thirties now, more tired than when we first met, but wiser, stronger, braver, truer together. We laugh, we dance, we sing each other's song. I write, and he proofreads. He is my coming home, my turning into my true self.

ABOUT THE AUTHOR

Photo © 2015 Joshua Drake

Cinelle Barnes is an essayist, memoirist, educator, and candlemaker with a BA in media studies in journalism from Hunter College and a master of fine arts in creative writing from Converse College. Books have been the one constant in her life—through her tumultuous childhood in the Philippines, her years living as an undocumented immigrant in New York City, her time as a new bride living in the American South, and as she completed her MFA program and began writing about her secrets. She lives between two states with her husband and daughter: New York, where she is always inspired to write, and South Carolina, where she can be close to the ocean. Find her online at www.cinellebarnes.com, and follow her on Instagram @cinellebarnesbooks.